麦格希 中英双语阅读文库

民间故事

【美】凯瑟琳·弗里德 (Katherine Follett) ●主编

刘慧　匡颖●译

麦格希中英双语阅读文库编委会●编

全国百佳图书出版单位
吉林出版集团股份有限公司

图书在版编目（CIP）数据

民间故事 /(美)凯瑟琳·弗里德
(Katherine Follett) 主编；麦格希中英双语阅读文库
编委会编；刘慧, 匡颖译. -- 2版. -- 长春：吉林出
版集团股份有限公司, 2018.3（2022.1重印）
（麦格希中英双语阅读文库）
ISBN 978-7-5581-4769-2

Ⅰ.①民… Ⅱ.①凯… ②麦… ③刘… ④匡… Ⅲ.
①英语—汉语—对照读物②民间故事—作品集—世界
Ⅳ.①H319.4：I

中国版本图书馆CIP数据核字(2018)第046091号

民间故事

编：	麦格希中英双语阅读文库编委会	
插　画：	齐 航　李延霞	
责任编辑：	孙琳琳	
封面设计：	冯冯翼	
开　本：	660mm×960mm　1/16	
字　数：	209千字	
印　张：	9.25	
版　次：	2018年3月第2版	
印　次：	2022年1月第2次印刷	

出　版：	吉林出版集团股份有限公司
发　行：	吉林出版集团外语教育有限公司
地　址：	长春市福祉大路5788号龙腾国际大厦B座7层
	邮编：130011
电　话：	总编办：0431-81629929
	发行部：0431-81629927 0431-81629921(Fax)
印　刷：	北京一鑫印务有限责任公司

ISBN 978-7-5581-4769-2　　　定价：35.00元

前言 *PREFACE*

英国思想家培根说过：阅读使人深刻。阅读的真正目的是获取信息，开拓视野和陶冶情操。从语言学习的角度来说，学习语言若没有大量阅读就如隔靴搔痒，因为阅读中的语言是最丰富、最灵活、最具表现力、最符合生活情景的，同时读物中的情节、故事引人入胜，进而能充分调动读者的阅读兴趣，培养读者的文学修养，至此，语言的学习水到渠成。

"麦格希中英双语阅读文库"在世界范围内选材，涉及科普、社会文化、文学名著、传奇故事、成长励志等多个系列，充分满足英语学习者课外阅读之所需，在阅读中学习英语、提高能力。

◎难度适中

本套图书充分照顾读者的英语学习阶段和水平，从读者的阅读兴趣出发，以难易适中的英语语言为立足点，选材精心、编排合理。

◎精品荟萃

本套图书注重经典阅读与实用阅读并举。既包含国内外脍炙人口、耳熟能详的美文，又包含科普、人文、故事、励志类等多学科的精彩文章。

◎功能实用

本套图书充分体现了双语阅读的功能和优势，充分考虑到读者课外阅读的方便，超出核心词表的词汇均出现在使其意义明显的语境之中，并标注释义。

鉴于编者水平有限，凡不周之处，谬误之处，皆欢迎批评教正。

我们真心地希望本套图书承载的文化知识和英语阅读的策略对提高读者的英语著作欣赏水平和英语运用能力有所裨益。

丛书编委会

Contents

Aladdin and the Wonderful Lamp

Chapter 1

Aladdin was the son of a poor *tailor*. His father tried to teach him the trade, but the boy was so lazy, he *refused* to do any work. Because Aladdin never lifted a finger, his father worked himself to exhaustion until he died. But even then, Aladdin would not change his lazy ways and played with the naughty boys in the street while his mother *spun* cotton.

When Aladdin was fifteen, a *magician* arrived in the kingdom. The

---

阿拉丁与神灯

第一章

阿拉丁是一个穷裁缝的儿子。他的父亲试图将生意传给他，可是阿拉丁很懒，拒绝付出任何努力。正因为阿拉丁在家里游手好闲，无所事事，所以父亲终日忙碌，直到死去。但即使在那种情况下，阿拉丁仍旧不愿改掉懒惰的生活方式，仍与调皮的孩子在街上嬉戏玩耍，而母亲在家辛苦地纺棉织布。

当阿拉丁15岁时，一个魔术师来到这个王国。魔术师在街上游荡，

---

tailor *n.* 裁缝　　　　　　　　　　refuse *v.* 拒绝
spin *v.* 纺织　　　　　　　　　　 magician *n.* 魔术师

magician wandered through the streets, looking for some foolish boy to trick. When he saw Aladdin, he *pounced on* him immediately.

"You there, your face looks *familiar*," he called. "Tell me who your father is."

"My father is Mustapha, the tailor. But he's been dead for two years," Aladdin replied.

"Oh, dear me, it can't be true! I've come all this way to see my brother, Mustapha, only to find out he is dead!" cried the magician. He hugged Aladdin close and *pretended* to *weep*. "And you, fine boy, must be my nephew. You've surely taken over your poor father's tailor shop."

"Bah!" said Aladdin. "I can't stand working! I prefer to play in the streets with my friends."

见到愚笨的孩子便戏弄一番。当他看到阿拉丁时，便立刻一把抓住了他。

"嗨，你看上去好面熟，"他喊道。"告诉我你父亲是谁。"

"我父亲叫穆斯塔法，是个裁缝。但是两年前，他去世了，"阿拉丁回答道。

"哦，天哪，怎么可能！我千辛万苦来到这里就是为了见我的哥哥，穆斯塔法，可他却早已不在人世！"魔术师大哭起来。他紧紧地搂住阿拉丁，假装哭泣。"可怜的孩子，那你就是我的侄子了。你一定接管了你父亲的裁缝店。"

"哼！"阿拉丁说道。"我才无法忍受那么辛苦的劳作呢！我要在街上和朋友玩耍。"

---

pounce on 一把抓住

pretend v. 假装

familiar adj. 熟悉的

weep v. 哭泣

"What? That's no good for a young boy. Let me make you an *offer*. If you come with me tomorrow, I'll buy a shop and make you a shopkeeper. That way, you can earn money without doing *labor*."

Aladdin liked the sound of that and agreed to follow his false uncle the next day.

Chapter 2

In the morning, the magician led Aladdin out of the city, across the countryside, and into the mountains. *Eventually* they came to a *ledge* on the edge of a cliff.

"Uncle, where is my shop? Why are we out here?" Aladdin asked.

"Gather some firewood, boy, and you'll be thankful you're here." So Aladdin gathered wood and built a small fire. The magician

---

"什么？这对一个年轻人来说可不是最佳的选择。让我来给你指点迷津吧。如果你明天跟随着我，我会给你一家店铺，让你成为主人。这样，你就可以不劳而获了。"

阿拉丁觉得这听起来不错，便答应第二天跟随着这个假冒的叔叔。

第二章

早晨，魔术师把阿拉丁带出了城，穿越村野，跨过高山。最后，他们来到了一个悬崖边上。

"叔叔，店铺在哪里？我们为什么要来到这里？"阿拉丁问道。

"拾些柴火，孩子，然后你就会发现，能来到这里，你是多么得幸

---

offer *n.* 提议　　　　　　　　　　　　labor *n.* 劳动
eventually *adv.* 最后　　　　　　　　　ledge *n.* 岩架

sprinkled incense over the flames, waved his hands, and murmured mysterious words. Before Aladdin's eyes, the earth opened up, revealing a stone with a *brass* ring attached. "Take hold of the ring and lift the stone!" ordered the magician.

Aladdin was quite afraid, for he was sure this was no ordinary uncle. He lifted the stone and saw a passageway leading down stone stairs into the darkness.

"Now, Nephew, you must do exactly as I say. Go down the stairs and into a golden hall, but do not touch the walls! Even brushing your sleeve against the gold will kill you instantly. At the end of the hall, you will come to a fruit *orchard* with a path leading to a small lamp sitting on a stone. Blow out the flame, empty the oil, and bring the lamp to me. I'll give you my ring, which will keep you from harm

运。"阿拉丁照做，并生了火。魔术师借着火焰点燃了香，挥动着手，嘴里默默地念叨。突然，在阿拉丁面前，大地裂开，出现了一块石头，上面有一枚铜戒。"快，抓住戒指，并搬起石头！"魔术师命令道。

阿拉丁很害怕，因为他意识到，叔叔不是一个普通人。他搬起石头，看到一条通道，沿着石梯直通向黑暗。

"侄子，现在你必须按我说的做。顺着梯子向下走，走到金色大厅，但是千万不要碰到墙壁！甚至袖子碰到了金子，也可能立刻要了你的命。在大厅尽头，你会看到一个果园，那里有一条路，你沿着路过去，会看到一块大石头，上面有一盏小油灯。吹灭火，倒空油，然后把灯给我带回

sprinkle *v.* 洒   incense *n.* 香
brass *n.* 黄铜   orchard *n.* 果树园

as long as you obey me."

Aladdin took the ring and went down the stairs, careful not to touch the golden walls of the beautiful hall. At the end of the hall, he entered a bright orchard with fruit trees bearing the most colorful, delicious fruit Aladdin had ever seen.

He could not resist *plucking* a bright red apple. As soon as he took it from the tree, the apple changed into a solid *ruby*! At the next tree, he plucked a bunch of golden grapes, which changed to a *cluster* of pearls. Lemons turned to diamonds, and limes to *emeralds*.

Aladdin gathered as much fruit as he could before following the path to the lamp. He piled the lamp on top of the treasure in his arms and returned to the stairs where his uncle waited.

来。我把戒指给你，只要你按我说的做，它就可以让你免受伤害。"

阿拉丁拿着戒指，沿梯子向下爬，小心翼翼地不去触碰美丽大厅的墙壁。在大厅尽头，他看到了一个绚烂的果园，树上正结着绚丽美味的果实。

他忍不住摘下一只红色的苹果。瞬间，这只苹果变成了红宝石！在另一棵树上，他摘下一串金色的葡萄，而它们变成了一串珍珠。柠檬变成了钻石，酸橙变成了翡翠。

在到达神灯那里之前，阿拉丁尽可能多地采集着水果。他手捧珠宝，把灯放在了最上面，返回到梯子处。

---

pluck *v.* 摘

cluster *n.* 串

ruby *n.* 红宝石

emerald *n.* 绿宝石

"Uncle, my load is heavy; help me up," he said.

"First give me the lamp!" demanded the magician.

"I told you, Uncle, my hands are full. I cannot give you anything until you help me."

"Foolish boy! Give me the lamp or stay down there forever!" The magician knew the lamp's magic would not work if he took it from someone by force.

"But Uncle!" *protested* Aladdin. Before he could finish, the magician *muttered* more magic words, and SLAM! the stone flew shut, locking Aladdin inside the cavern.

Aladdin called and called, but his uncle would not answer. Finally he decided to *pray*, but when he put his hands together, he accidentally rubbed the magician's ring. Instantly, a frightful *genie*

"叔叔，太沉了，快来帮我上去，"他喊道。

"先把灯交给我！"魔术师命令道。

"叔叔，真的，我抽不出手来。如果你不帮我，我没办法给你。"

"愚蠢！快把神灯给我，否则你就永远待在下面吧！"魔术师知道，通过武力得到神灯，它是不会发挥神效的。

"不，叔叔！"阿拉丁反抗道。可还没等他说完，魔术师又念起咒语。砰！石头瞬时飞了起来，封上了裂缝，把阿拉丁困在洞穴里。

阿拉丁喊着叫着，可是叔叔不会回应。最后，他决定祈祷。当他双手合十，他意外地摩擦到了魔术师的戒指。立刻，一个神怪站在他面前。

---

protest *v.* 抗议
pray *v.* 祈祷

mutter *v.* 嘀咕
genie *n.* 神怪

stood before him. "What would you have? I am the slave of whoever wears the ring."

Aladdin was terrified, but he immediately replied, "Bring me home!" In no time, he stood at his front door, his worried mother weeping with joy to see him. Aladdin was *starving*, and he begged his mother to sell one of the treasures—the *dusty* lamp, perhaps—for food.

His mother began to polish the lamp with an old rag, and another enormous genie appeared. "What would you have? I am the *slave* of whoever owns the lamp."

His mother was terrified, but Aladdin knew what to do. "Bring us a satisfying feast!" he shouted. In an instant, the genie brought dozens of solid silver trays *overflowing* with food. Buttery rolls,

---

"你想要什么？我将听从任何戴戒指的人的命令。"

阿拉丁吓坏了，但他立即回答，"带我回家！"很快，阿拉丁站在了家门口，焦虑万分的母亲看到儿子，也喜极而泣。阿拉丁饿极了，他要母亲卖掉一样值钱的东西——那盏满是灰尘的灯，也许——能换点食物。

母亲开始用抹布擦拭那盏灯，又一个神怪出现了。"你想要什么？我会听从任何拥有这盏灯的主人的命令。"

母亲吓坏了，但阿拉丁知道该做什么。"我要一桌丰盛的美食！"他喊道。瞬间，神怪带来了许多用银盘盛满的食物。桌上摆满了黄油卷，赏心悦目的松糕和热气腾腾的烤肉。当阿拉丁和母亲用完餐后，桌上剩下的

---

starve *v.* 饿死

slave *n.* 奴隶

dusty *adj.* 满是灰尘的

overflow *v.* 充满

delectable pastries, and steaming roasts filled their table. When Aladdin and his mother finished, enough food still remained for many days. They would never be hungry again. When the food ran out, they sold a piece of beautiful silverware or one of the trays for more.

Chapter 3

They would have lived like this forever if Aladdin had not been on the street when he heard the town crier shouting, "Back to your houses, all! *Shutter* your windows! Princess Buddir will go to the bath!" No one was allowed to see the Sultan's daughter without her veil. Aladdin hid himself behind the wall of the bathhouse, eager to see the princess's face. When she came by with her *servants*, Aladdin was so struck by her beauty, he *vowed* he would marry her.

"Have you lost your senses?" cried his mother when he told her his plans.

食物足够吃上许多天。他们再也不会挨饿了。当食物吃光，他们卖掉了这些漂亮银餐具或任何一个盘子，换来了更多食物。

第三章

也许他们的日子可以一直这样过下去，直到阿拉丁来到街上，听到城镇传达公告的人在喊，"都回到屋子里去！关上窗！公主卜朵要沐浴了！"没有人可以见到摘掉面纱的公主。阿拉丁躲在浴房墙后面，期待着见一眼公主的脸。当公主在仆人的陪同下出现的时候，阿拉丁被她的美貌深深地打动，便发誓一定要娶她为妻。

"你疯了吗？"当他把计划告诉母亲时，母亲喊道。

---

delectable *adj.* 好吃的；赏心悦目的
servant *n.* 仆人

shutter *v.* 关上
vow *v.* 发誓

"Only my heart," Aladdin replied. "Take this silver tray from our meal and load it with fruit from the cavern. Wrap it carefully in rags and take it to the Sultan to ask for his daughter's hand in marriage."

Though she *grumbled* that a tailor's wife would never be allowed to see the Sultan, Aladdin's mother piled the tray with *gleaming* jewels and wrapped it in rags. The Sultan's guards would have thrown her out, but the Sultan was curious as to what was hidden inside the *bundle*. He ordered Aladdin's mother into his hall.

Aladdin's mother bowed low, holding up the rag bundle, which was scarcely *distinguishable* from her clothing. "Sultan, my son begs for your daughter's hand in marriage."

"只有她能打动我的心，"阿拉丁回答道。"拿着这银盘，把它盛满山洞里的水果。再用破布把它包好，然后带给苏丹，请求他把女儿嫁给我。"

母亲一边抱怨着裁缝的妻子是不允许见苏丹的，一边将闪闪发光的珠宝放到盘子里，用破布包裹好。苏丹的门卫原本是可以把她扔出去的，可是国王如此好奇，想知道包裹里到底藏着什么东西。他命令让阿拉丁的母亲进去。

阿拉丁的母亲深深地鞠了一躬，手里拿着那个破包裹，破旧得如同她身上的衣服。"国王陛下，我儿子请求您把女儿嫁给他。"

---

grumble *v.* 抱怨　　　　　　　gleaming *adj.* 闪烁的
bundle *n.* 包裹　　　　　　　distinguishable *adj.* 可区别的

The Sultan burst out laughing. "Even if I allowed it, my daughter would be *insulted* to live with someone as poor as your son. But before I *toss* you out, unwrap your bundle and show me what you have brought."

Aladdin's mother unwrapped the package, and the enormous jewels *glittered* in the *sunlit* hall. The Sultan's jaw fell open as he admired a gold pear, for he had never seen such treasures.

"I am very impressed. Perhaps your son is worthy after all. But before I allow my daughter to marry him, he must truly prove his worth. Tell him he has seven days to deliver forty trays of these same gems. Each tray must be solid gold. Each gold tray must be carried by two slaves, and each slave must be dressed in the richest

---

　　国王突然大笑起来。"即便我同意了，让我的女儿和像你儿子这样的穷小子生活在一起，简直就是一种耻辱。但是，在我把你扔出去之前，打开你的包裹，让我看看你带来了什么。"

　　阿拉丁的母亲打开包裹，硕大的珠宝在金碧辉煌的大厅更加熠熠生辉。国王从没见过如此漂亮的宝贝，当他拿起一枚金梨欣赏时，他目瞪口呆。

　　"我很欣赏。也许，你的儿子能够配得上我的女儿。不过，在我允许他娶我女儿之前，我要考验考验他。去吧，告诉他，他有7天的时间准备出40盘同样的珍宝。每个盘子都必须是纯金的。每个盘子都要由两个奴隶

---

insult *v.* 侮辱　　　　　　　　　　　　　toss *v.* 投；抛
glitter *v.* 闪闪发光　　　　　　　　　　sunlit *adj.* 阳光照射的

clothing."

Aladdin's mother went back to her son and told him what the Sultan had said. Aladdin laughed, for the power of the lamp could get him anything. Instantly, the genie produced a train of eighty slaves carrying trays of gold and jewels. A crowd gathered to watch them *march* to the Sultan's palace behind Aladdin's ragged mother.

"Again, you have impressed me," the Sultan said. "But I must know that he will keep my daughter happy. Tell your son to have a *splendid* palace ready for her by the end of the week."

In a flash, Aladdin ordered the genie to build a *magnificent* palace in the garden across from the Sultan's window. The genie even ran a soft red *carpet* from the door of Aladdin's palace to the door of

---

托着，并且每个奴隶都要穿着最华丽的衣裳。"

阿拉丁的母亲回到家，把国王的话告诉了儿子。阿拉丁笑了，因为神灯可以帮助他得到一切。立刻，神怪变出了80个奴隶，手里托着盛满金银珠宝的盘子。人们聚集起来看着他们，在衣衫褴褛的母亲后面，朝着国王的宫殿走去。

"不错，我又很满意，"国王说道。"可是我必须知道他是否会让我的女儿幸福。去吧，告诉你的儿子，在本周末之前，准备好豪华的宫殿。"

没用多久，阿拉丁命令神怪在国王窗下的花园里造了一座宏伟的宫

---

march *v.* 前进

magnificent *adj.* 宏伟的

splendid *adj.* 辉煌的

carpet *n.* 毯子

the Sultan's. Aladdin himself, dressed in the finest silk, rode to the Sultan's door on a horse more beautiful than any in the Sultan's *stables*.

"It would be unfair to my daughter if I did not allow her to marry such a worthy man," said the Sultan.

And so it was that Aladdin and the princess were married. All the kingdom came to the wedding *procession*. Musicians led the Princess Buddir down the carpet toward Aladdin's palace, and four hundred torches lit the street as bright as day. Inside Aladdin's palace, they ate a *sumptuous feast* on solid silver plates. It was the most joyful occasion the kingdom could remember, and Aladdin and Buddir had happiness for many years.

殿。神怪还在阿拉丁宫殿通往国王宫殿的路上铺了一条松软的红色地毯。阿拉丁本人，也身着真丝薄纱，骑着马来到国王面前，这匹马要胜过国王马厩里的任何一匹。

"如果我再阻止女儿嫁给一个这样如此有出息的人，那就太不公正了。"国王说道。

阿拉丁和公主顺理成章地结为夫妻。整个王国的人们都来到婚礼列队中。音乐家引领着公主踏着地毯来到阿拉丁的宫殿，400把火炬把街道照亮得如白昼。在阿拉丁的宫殿里，他们品尝着纯银盘子里盛满的美食。这是令所有人都感到最难忘最兴奋的场合。从此，阿拉丁和公主过着幸福的生活。

---

stable *n.* 马棚
sumptuous *adj.* 奢侈的

procession *n.* 行列
feast *n.* 盛宴

Chapter 4

They would have lived like this forever, but Aladdin loved riding among the streets of the city throwing gold to everyone he met. This made him quite famous. Soon, the magician heard of this boy who seemed to have riches as if by magic. He knew Aladdin had stolen his ring and lamp to gain his wealth.

The magician *disguised* himself as a *peddler*, filled a basket with shiny lamps, and came to the palace door while Aladdin was out. "Who will exchange old lamps for new ones?" he called. Buddir *peeked* out the window.

"Won't Aladdin be surprised when he finds a shiny new lamp instead of that dull one he keeps in his *chamber*?" She took the magic

---

第四章

他们的日子原本可以一直这样过下去，可是阿拉丁喜欢在城里走街串巷，向他遇到的人分发金币。这也使他家喻户晓。不久，魔术师听说了此事。他知道一定是阿拉丁偷走了戒指和神灯，才能获得如此财富。

魔术师化装成小贩，篮子里装满了崭新的油灯。当阿拉丁出门后，便在宫殿外面叫卖。"旧灯换新灯喽？"他喊道。公主探出窗外，一看究竟。

"把橱柜里的旧油灯换成崭新的油灯，阿拉丁一定会感到惊喜的！"她把神灯从阿拉丁的房间拿了出来，递给了小贩。立刻，魔术师擦拭神

---

disguise *v.* 假扮

peek *v.* 瞥见

peddler *n.* 小贩

chamber *n.* 房间

lamp from Aladdin's room and brought it to the peddler. Immediately, the magician rubbed the lamp and *summoned* the genie.

"What would you have? I am the slave of whoever owns the lamp."

"Take this princess and her palace and servants and send us all to Africa!" the magician cried. With a flash, the palace vanished.

When the Sultan looked out of his window, he gasped in horror. His daughter's palace had vanished in a *puff* of smoke! He ordered that Aladdin be brought before him.

The Sultan *raged*. "Whatever *sorcery* you used to produce your riches has made my daughter disappear! If you cannot bring her back in five days, I'll chop off your head!"

灯，召唤神怪出现。

　　"你想要什么？我会听从任何拥有这灯的主人的命令。"

　　"把这位公主和她的宫殿及仆人，还有我，带到非洲去！"魔术师命令道。一眨眼的工夫，宫殿便消失了。

　　此时，国王透过窗户看到了发生的一切，他惊讶地吸了一口气。女儿的宫殿伴随着一股烟儿瞬间消失了！他命令立刻传见阿拉丁。

　　国王大怒。"你用魔法变出的财富却让我的女儿消失了！如果5天内，你不能找回我的女儿，我就处置你！"

---

summon *v.* 召唤　　　　　　　　　　puff *n.* 一股
rage *v.* 发怒　　　　　　　　　　　sorcery *n.* 巫术

Aladdin pleaded his innocence, but the Sultan would hear none of it. Sadder than he had ever been, Aladdin wandered the city for three days. He asked everyone if they had seen his princess. On the fourth day, he decided to pray, and he rubbed the magic ring, which he had almost forgotten about.

"What would you have? I am the slave of whoever wears the ring."

"Please, return my palace as it was!"

"Only the Genie of the Lamp can undo what the Genie of the Lamp has done," the genie answered.

"Then take me to my palace," Aladdin said. Before he could *blink*, Aladdin stood at the front door of his palace, which now sat in a lonely desert in Africa. He *snuck* inside and *reunited* with his Princess Buddir, and they both *shed* tears of joy.

阿拉丁努力乞求，澄清自己是清白的，可是国王什么听不进去。阿拉丁如此得悲伤，他在城里逛了三天三夜。他逢人就问，是否见到了公主。第四天，他决定祈祷，他搓着那枚几乎被抛之脑后的神戒。

"你想要什么？我会听从任何拥有这枚神戒的主人的命令。"

"求你让我的宫殿回到我的身边！"

"只有神灯神怪才能撤销他的行为，"神怪回答道。

"那么，带我去我的宫殿，"阿拉丁说道。眨眼工夫，阿拉丁已经站在了他的宫殿门口，此时，宫殿正坐落在非洲荒芜的沙漠上。他溜了进去，看到了公主，他们为能再次相聚都喜极而泣。

---

blink *v.* 眨眼
reunite *v.* 重聚

sneak *v.* 溜
shed *v.* 流出

"I have a plan to get our lamp back," whispered Aladdin. He gave Buddir a *pouch* filled with a *potion* that made its victims slow and sleepy.

Buddir then invited the magician to eat with her. Flattered by her sudden kindness, the magician allowed the princess to pour his drink. She secretly added the powder, and soon the magician was nodding in his soup.

"My dear," said Buddir, "doesn't it seem awfully dark in here?"

The magician's eyelids were half-closed, so it did seem dark to him. "Why yes, it does," he mumbled.

"Why don't you give me that old lamp you carry around, so we may dine by its *flame*?" The magician, *numbed* by the potion, handed

---

"我有一个找回神灯的办法，"阿拉丁小声地说道。他给了公主一个装满安眠药的小袋子。

随后，公主邀请魔术师共进晚餐。得到公主的款待，兴奋之余，魔术师让公主斟满了他的酒杯。公主就在这时偷偷地投下了药，没过多久，魔术师一边喝着汤，一边开始昏昏欲睡。

"亲爱的，"公主说道，"这里是不是太黑了？"

魔术师的眼皮已经半合上了，所以他一定感觉很黑。"是呀，确实很黑。"他喃喃道。

"那为什么不把你那盏神灯拿出来，这样我们也可以伴着火光进餐

---

pouch *n.* 小袋子

flame *n.* 火焰

potion *n.* 一剂

numb *v.* 使麻木

her the magic lamp. She summoned the genie immediately.

"Take me and Aladdin and my palace back to the Sultan's *kingdom*, and leave this *horrid* magician in the desert where he will never find his way out!" she ordered. The genie did as she asked, and they were all returned to their home safe and sound.

The Sultan was so pleased to see his daughter again, he made Aladdin the heir to his *throne*. After the Sultan passed on the *crown*, Aladdin and Buddir ruled the kingdom for many happy years.

呀？"此时，魔术师已被药剂麻醉，便将灯递给了公主。公主随即把灯神召唤了出来。

"快，带我和阿拉丁，还有我们的宫殿回到苏丹身边！把这个讨厌的魔术师丢在这片沙漠里，不要让他找到回去的路！"她命令道。灯神执行命令，他们便又平安地回到了他们的家。

国王再次见到女儿，十分高兴，他把王位传给了阿拉丁。阿拉丁继位后，统治着这个王国，和公主过着幸福的生活。

---

kingdom *n.* 王国
throne *n.* 王位

horrid *adj.* 讨厌的
crown *n.* 王冠

2

Robin Hood Wins the Sheriff's Golden Arrow

Introduction

Robin Hood's life in Sherwood Forest was very pleasant for those who were not afraid of *roughing* it. The *Merry* Men loved the trees, birds, and animals in the forest. They built shelters of bark and logs to keep out the rain, and they did not mind that there were no houses, soft beds, or fine chairs and tables. When it wasn't raining, they slept on *deerskins* under the stars. The band cooked over a *roaring* fire next to a big tree and ate sitting on the ground.

罗宾汉赢得了郡长的金箭

引子

罗宾汉在舍伍德森林的生活非常快乐，在他身边的人都是些生活得粗枝大叶的人。他的伙伴们"快活人"热爱森林里的树木、小鸟和各种动物。他们住在用树皮和圆木搭建的小屋里避雨，没有房子和舒适的床，也没有精致的桌椅，这些他们都不在乎。不下雨的时候，他们就睡在鹿皮上，直面星空。这一群人在一棵大树旁生火煮饭，然后坐在地上吃。

---

rough v. 使粗糙
deerskin n. 鹿皮

merry adj. 欢乐的
roaring adj. 兴旺的

More than a hundred men made up Robin Hood's band. These rough outlaws with kind hearts were devoted to Robin Hood and obeyed his every word. Robin needed only to lift his *bugle* to his lips and play a note, and the men would appear. They were the best *archers*, wrestlers, and swordsmen in all of England, and they got better as they practiced their skills daily. Robin Hood was the best of all the archers in the land; his aim was true and swift. Even King Richard admired Robin's *bold* skill with a bow and arrow.

Robin and his men stole from the rich lords and gave their treasure back to the poor. Times were bad in England, for the French had conquered the whole country. They left the English king, King Richard, in power, but ruled the land while he was at war. These cruel lords got rich taxing the poor, sometimes taking all a family owned. They also were in league with *corrupt* churchmen, who took

---

罗宾汉的手下共有100多人。这些人不在乎世俗法律的约束，他们心地善良，对罗宾汉很忠诚，服从他的指挥。罗宾只需拿起号角吹一声，这些人就会出现。这群人里有全英格兰最出色的弓箭手、摔跤手和剑客；而且他们每天练习，水平越来越高。罗宾汉是其中最出色的弓箭手；他瞄准目标总是准确、神速。即使是国王理查德都羡慕罗宾汉的弓箭水平。

罗宾和他的手下偷走贵族们的财富分给穷人。英格兰当时情况很糟，因为法国人征服了英国。他们留下英国国王理查德执政，但在他外出征战的时候统治了英国。这些残暴的贵族们向穷人们征了很高的税，有时候一个家庭交完税就一无所有。他们还和腐败的教士联手，因为教士会利用人

---

bugle *n.* 喇叭
bold *adj.* 显著的

archer *n.* 弓箭手
corrupt *adj.* 腐败的

advantage of the faith of the common people. As a child, Robin Hood had seen many of his friends' and neighbors' lives ruined. He vowed to grow up and make things right. He became an outlaw, though the laws he broke were *unjust* ones. Robin Hood's men made feasts to lure the *lords* who traveled the roads near the forest. When the lords came to feast, Robin and his men took the gold the lords had stolen and gave it back to the English people. To his enemies, Robin and his men were robbers; to the common *folk*, they were heroes.

The Sheriff of Nottingham

The Sheriff of Nottingham hated Robin Hood more than any other lord hated him. The Sheriff was a *cruel* man with no kindness in his heart. He wanted nothing more than to catch Robin Hood and hang him.

们的信仰来做坏事。罗宾汉小时候就见过自己的朋友和邻居的生活被毁。他发誓长大以后要伸张正义。后来他成了社会上的反叛者，但他所违反的法律都是不公正的法律。罗宾汉的伙伴们做好大餐吸引在森林边路过的贵族们。在贵族们吃大餐的时候，罗宾和他的朋友们会抢走贵族们偷来的金子，还给英国百姓。对于敌人来说，罗宾汉和他的伙伴们是强盗；对于老百姓来说，他们是英雄。

诺丁汉郡的郡长

诺丁汉郡的郡长比任何一个贵族更憎恨罗宾汉。这个郡长很残忍，心无善念。他最想做的事就是抓住罗宾汉，绞死他。

---

unjust *adj.* 不公正的
folk *n.* 百姓

lord *n.* 贵族
cruel *adj.* 残忍的

Time after time, Robin got away, and the Sheriff only grew angrier and more *spiteful*. One day he sent a *stout* guard with a *warrant* to catch Robin Hood. Robin met the guard on the road and led him to a feast in the forest. The guard ate so much, he fell asleep with a belly full of food and drink. While the guard slept, Robin stole the warrant right out of his pocket. Without a warrant the guard couldn't arrest Robin Hood and his men, and he had to go back to the Sheriff empty handed. Still, the *furious* Sheriff of Nottingham would not give up his hunt for Robin.

He knew it was no use sending more guards, no matter how strong they were. The Sheriff had no choice but to trick Robin into leaving the forest.

"I've got it," said the Sheriff of Nottingham, wearing a sour look

---

罗宾一次又一次地逃脱，郡长就越来越愤怒，怀恨在心。一天，郡长派了一个强壮的卫兵带着逮捕令去捉拿罗宾汉。罗宾在路上遇见了这个卫兵，就请他去森林吃大餐。卫兵吃得太饱，喝得太多，吃完就呼呼睡着了。卫兵睡着的时候，罗宾从他的口袋里偷出了逮捕令。没有了逮捕令，卫兵就不能逮捕罗宾和他的手下了，他只好空手回到郡长那里。但这个怒火冲天的郡长仍然没有放弃逮捕罗宾的计划。

他明白让卫兵去抓他是没有用的，卫兵再强壮也没用。郡长没有什么妙计，只好想办法骗罗宾离开森林。

"有办法了，"郡长面露敌意地说。"我略施小计就能捉住他。我

---

spiteful *adj.* 怀恨的
warrant *n.* 逮捕令

stout *adj.* 结实的
furious *adj.* 狂怒的

on his face. "I'll catch him by trickery. I'll hold a great archery festival and have the best archers in England come here to shoot for the prize of a gold-covered arrow. Surely that will draw Robin Hood and his men so I can arrest and hang them."

Robin Hood and his men prepared to go to the archery contest, but they didn't wear the green suits they wore in the forest. Instead they dressed in *disguise*. Some dressed as *barefoot* monks, some as traders, others as farmers and peasants. Robin Hood was the hardest to *recognize*, dressed from head to toe in *tattered* beggar's clothes.

Yet his loyal men were worried and begged Robin not to go. "This archery contest is just a trap for the Sheriff to lure you to your death. The Sheriff of Nottingham and his guards will know you by your hair

---

要举办一场盛大的箭术比赛,让英格兰最好的弓箭手都来参赛,冠军将获得一只镀金的箭。这样罗宾汉和他的手下一定会被吸引来,我就可以逮捕他,再绞死他。"

罗宾汉和他的伙伴们准备好去参加箭术大赛,但他们没有穿平时在森林里穿的绿色衣服。他们都穿了不同的衣服好让别人认不出。有些人打扮成赤脚的和尚,有些人打扮成商人,其他人则打扮成农民或乡下人。罗宾汉的装扮是最难认出来的,他从头到脚穿着一身破烂的乞丐服装。

但是他那些忠诚的手下还是很担心,不让他去参赛。"箭术大赛肯定是郡长设下的陷阱,要害死你。郡长和卫兵们看你的头发和眼睛还是能认

---

disguise *n.* 伪装
recognize *v.* 认出

barefoot *adj.* 赤足的
tattered *adj.* 破烂的

and eyes, even if you wear different clothes. Please, please don't go to the contest, Robin Hood."

Robin Hood just laughed at his band's concern for him. "Why, as to my yellow hair, I can color that with *walnut stain*. As to my eyes, I can cover one of them with a *patch* so my face will not be seen in the crowd. The Sheriff of Nottingham and his guards don't scare me—in fact, a bit of danger will make it all the more fun."

The Archery Festival

So the brave Robin Hood left for the contest wearing rags like a beggar. The field where the contest was to be held was quite a sight. Workers had set up rows and rows of benches for the viewers to sit on. *Glee* filled the hearts of the people in the crowd, and they wore their very best clothes. All the cruel and wealthy lords were dressed

---

出你，换了衣服也没用。求你了罗宾汉，求你别去参赛了。"

对于伙伴们的担忧，罗宾汉只是大笑。"为什么不去呢，要是担心我的黄头发，我可以染成茶色。要是担心我的眼睛，我可以戴一只眼罩，这样混在人群里就不会被认出来了。郡长和那群卫兵根本吓不到我——其实，带点危险会更好玩。"

箭术大赛

这样，无畏的罗宾汉就化装成乞丐去参赛了。比赛地点视角很宽广。工人们搭建起一排排的凳子给观众们坐。人们都穿着漂亮的衣服，心里欢快无比。那些阴险富有的贵族们打扮得像一群风鸟。郡长穿着紫色的天鹅

---

walnut *n.* 茶色

patch *n.* 眼罩

stain *n.* 染色剂

glee *n.* 欢乐

like birds of *paradise*. The Sheriff had on purple velvet while his lady wore blue velvet, both *trimmed* with pure white fur, and they wore broad gold chains around their necks. If their faces had been kind, they would have looked beautiful, but their faces were full of pride and hate.

The Sheriff looked high and low for Robin Hood. There stood Robin in his beggar's clothes not ten feet from the Sheriff, but still the Sheriff did not recognize him. The targets were eighty yards away from where the archers were to stand. They were so far off, it was difficult to make out the circles. *Dozens* and dozens of archers took turns shooting just one arrow. The ten best archers, those who had actually hit the *target*, were then to shoot two arrows each. The three best of those ten would each have three shots, and the prize

---

绒，他的夫人穿着蓝色的天鹅绒。两件外套都有着纯白的毛边，两人的脖子上都带着大金项链。如果他们面容和善，看起来一定很漂亮，但他们的脸上满是不屑与恨意。

郡长四处张望寻找罗宾汉。穿着乞丐衣服的罗宾汉就站在离郡长不到十英尺的地方，但郡长还是没认出他。比赛的靶子设立在离弓箭手们80码远的地方。离得太远，弓箭手们看不清靶子上的圆环。弓箭手一批批上前，第一轮每人只有一次射箭的机会。射到靶子的有十人，这前十名弓箭手接下来每人有两次射击机会。其中的前三名下一轮每人有三次射击机

---

paradise *n.* 天堂
dozen *n.* 十二个

trim *v.* 点缀
target *n.* 靶子

would go to the archer whose arrow landed nearest to the center of the target.

Finally it was time for the ten best archers to *vie* for the prize. The Sheriff *glared* at the ten men. "I was sure Robin Hood would be one of the final archers," he said to the guard at his side. "Couldn't one of these men be Robin Hood dressed in a disguise?"

"No, sir," said the man-at-arms. "Six of them I know well; they are the best archers in England. There's Gill o' the Red Cap, Diccon Cruikshank, Adam o' the Dell, William o' Leslie, Hubert o' Cloud, and Swithin o' Hertford. Of the other four, one is too tall, one is too short, and one is too *lean* to be Robin Hood. That leaves only the ragged beggar, and his hair and *beard* are much too dark to be Robin Hood's, and he is blind in one eye. Robin Hood is safe in Sherwood

---

会，谁的箭离靶心最近谁就会成为获胜者。

最后到了前十名的弓箭手争夺大奖的时刻了。郡长盯着这十个人看。"我相信罗宾汉一定在这十个人中，"他对身边的卫兵说。"会不会其中一个是乔装打扮的罗宾汉？"

"不会的，郡长，"这名卫兵答到。"有六个人我认识，他们是英格兰最好的弓箭手。来自红帽子的吉尔，德尔的迪肯和亚当，莱斯利的威廉，克莱德的胡伯特和哈特福德的斯卫金。其他的四个人和罗宾汉相比，一个太高，一个太矮，一个太瘦。那就只剩下那个穿得破烂的乞丐了，他的头发和胡子颜色比罗宾汉深得多，还有一只眼睛瞎了，不会是罗宾汉。

---

vie *v.* 竞争
lean *adj.* 瘦的

glare *v.* 注视
beard *n.* 胡须

Forest."

The guard was glad Robin hadn't fallen for the trap, for he didn't want to see Robin harmed. Robin Hood had lots of friends among the common people, and even the Sheriff's own guards had helped him get away many times. But even his *loyal* friends could not spot Robin on this day.

The ten top archers aimed and let their *quills* fly. The crowd watched in *awe* as each of the arrows struck near the center of the target.

The time came for the last three archers to raise their *bows*. Gill o' the Red Cap's first arrow struck only an inch from the center. His second and third were even closer. Then Robin Hood, who looked to everyone like the poorest beggar in England, shot his arrow to

---

罗宾汉肯定舒服地待在舍伍德森林里呢。"

卫兵很高兴罗宾汉没相信郡长的诡计，因为他也不想看到罗宾受伤。罗宾汉不仅在老百姓中交了很多朋友，连郡长身边的卫兵们都帮他逃脱了好多次。但是即使是他很忠诚的朋友，这一天也没能认出罗宾。

十名弓箭手瞄准，开始射箭。每次箭接近靶心的时候，人们都惊叹无比。

最后，到了前三名弓箭手比赛的时候了。吉尔射出的第一箭离靶心只有一英寸。其余两箭离靶心更近。然后是罗宾汉——他看起来好像是英格

---

loyal *adj.* 忠诚的
awe *n.* 敬畏

quill *n.* 箭
bow *n.* 弓

the very center. The crowd *gasped*. Adam o' the Dell still had yet to shoot, but he unstrung his bow when he saw the beggar's arrow strike. "I've been an archer for eighty years," said the man. "And I will never be able to do better than that."

And so the tattered beggar won the prized gold-covered arrow. But the Sheriff's face was *scrunched* and sour when the time came to give it to him. "You are the best archer I have ever seen," he said. "You shoot even better than that coward Robin Hood, who dared not show his face today. I will pay you well if you join my service."

"I will not," said the ragged stranger. Robin Hood left quickly under the *gaze* of a spiteful Sheriff. But the Sheriff's words got to Robin as he walked back to the wood. "I just can't bear to have him think I am a *coward*," he said to Little John, his right-hand man. "I

兰最贫穷的乞丐——三箭都正中靶心。人们都倒吸了一口气。本来轮到亚当射箭，但他看完乞丐的箭术之后，解开了弓弦。"我做射手80年了，"他说。"但我永远不可能像他射得那么准。"

这样，衣衫褴褛的乞丐赢得了那只镀金的箭。但是当郡长把奖颁给他的时候，表情却是扭曲、刻薄的。"你是我见过的最好的弓箭手，"他说。"你的箭术甚至比罗宾汉还要好。他今天根本不敢露面。如果你愿意到我这来当差，我会付给你一大笔钱。"

"我不会来的，"这位穿着破烂的陌生人说。罗宾汉在郡长仇恨的眼神下快速离开了。但当他回到树林以后，郡长的话却在他耳边响起来。

---

gasp *v.* 抽气
gaze *n.* 凝视

scrunch *v.* 使弯曲
coward *n.* 懦夫

wish there were a way to let the Sheriff know I am the person who won his fine gold-covered arrow."

The Message

The Sheriff was *glum* that night at the rich supper table with his wife. "I thought I could catch that thief with this contest," he said to her.

"I guess Robin Hood was too much of a coward to show his face." Right then, a *shaft crashed* through the window and stuck straight into the roast. The Sheriff *unfolded* the note that was stuck to the arrow. It read that the beggar at the contest had been none other than Robin Hood. The note instructed him to look closely at the arrow. When he did, the Sheriff realized it was one of his own

---

"我不能忍受他认为我是个懦夫。"他对他的得力助手小约翰说。"我希望用什么方法能让郡长知道，我才是赢得了他那只金箭的人。"

消息

那天晚上，郡长闷闷不乐地和他的夫人坐在餐桌旁。"我本以为举办这个比赛能抓住那个贼呢，"他对他夫人说。

"我猜罗宾汉就是懦夫一个，根本不敢露面。"就在这时，一只箭杆穿透窗户，正好钉在烤肉上。郡长打开飞进来的箭上别着的纸条。纸条上说参加比赛的乞丐不是别人，正是罗宾汉。纸条上还说让他好好看看这支箭。郡长一看，这正是他自己的箭——正是他镀了金后当作奖品的箭。罗

---

glum *adj.* 闷闷不乐的
crash *v.* 冲

shaft *n.* 箭杆
unfold *v.* 打开

arrows—the very same arrow he had covered in gold and given as the prize. Robin Hood's men had *scraped* off the gold and kept it. The *duped* sheriff *upended* the table and *stormed* off, madder than he had ever been in his whole life.

宾汉的手下刮去了镀金，把箭留了下来。上当的郡长大发雷霆，推翻了桌子，他一辈子从没发过这么大的火。

---

scrap *v.* 削
upend *v.* 使倒放

duped *adj.* 上当的
storm *v.* 气冲冲地走

3

How Little John Joined Robin Hood

Introduction

One day when Robin Hood was a young boy, he returned to his old neighborhood to hear news of his friends. But many of his friends had been thrown out of their homes, arrested, or hanged. The French had *conquered* England, and they ruled over the common people with an iron *fist*. Though the English king was still on the throne, he was often at war, and the French ruled in his *absence*. They *taxed* families until they starved. Then they stole their land and gave it to their corrupt friends in the church.

小约翰是怎样加入罗宾汉的

引子

罗宾汉小时候的一天，去他的老邻居那里打听他朋友的消息。但他的许多朋友都被迫离开家园，有的被逮捕，有的被绞死。法国人征服了英格兰，用铁拳统治了英国民众。尽管英国国王仍然在位，但他经常外出作战。他不在的时候法国人就来统治英格兰。他们向普通家庭征重税，英国国内民不聊生。他们还偷窃土地，分给他们在教堂里的腐败朋友。

---

conquer *v.* 征服
absence *n.* 不在

fist *n.* 拳头
tax *v.* 收税

From that day, Robin Hood vowed he would bring *justice* back to the land. Since the rich stole from the poor, Robin would steal back from the rich and return the money to the common people. He cleverly hid himself in Sherwood Forest where he was safe from the lords who hated him. He stole only from people who dared to travel near the wood. But his name quickly became famous, and English people everywhere loved him very much. Men from all over decided to join Robin Hood's *quest*. Soon he had a large band of men who lived with him in the forest. Robin Hood's men were more loyal to him than they had ever been to their cruel French lords.

The Merry Men, as they became known, lived *entirely* outdoors, hunting for their food, cooking over a fire, and sleeping under the stars. They spent their days practicing archery, *wrestling*, and sword

---

　　从那时起，罗宾汉就发誓要夺回正义。穷人的东西被富人偷走，罗宾就从富人手里偷回来还给老百姓。他机智地藏身于舍伍德森林，痛恨他的贵族们也拿他没办法。他只偷那些敢于走近林子的人。但是他很快名声大噪，英国人民都很热爱他。人们从四面八方涌来，要加入罗宾汉的队伍。很快，就有一大群人同他一起住在森林里。罗宾汉的手下人对他无比忠诚，比之前对那些残忍的法国贵族们要忠诚一百倍。

　　人们把这群人叫作"快活人"，他们完全住在户外，打猎为食，露天生火，席地而睡，天空为被。他们每天练习射箭、摔跤、击剑，成了英格

---

justice　*n.* 公正
entirely　*adv.* 完全地

quest　*n.* 探索
wrestling　*n.* 摔跤

fighting until they were the strongest men in England. There were only two types of *lawful* men left in the land: wealthy men who hated Robin Hood, and honest and good men who envied Robin Hood's bravery and freedom. Tales of Robin's deeds are still told to this day, including this one.

John Little

This is the story of how Robin Hood gained his *right-hand man* and dearest friend, Little John. John Little was his real name before he joined Robin Hood's band. He was the tallest and strongest man who ever walked through the kingdom. Unlike most men, he was not loyal to anyone, neither to the lords nor to the *outlaws*. He was such a brave fighter that he felt safest when he was by himself. When Robin Hood first saw him, John Little was *strolling* on the edge of the forest

---

兰最有本领的人。英格兰人分为两类：憎恨罗宾汉的有钱人和敬仰罗宾汉自由勇敢的好人们。罗宾汉的故事流传至今，下面的故事就是其中一个。

约翰·利特尔

这个故事讲的是罗宾汉是怎样使约翰·利特尔加入的，而且还成了他的得力助手和最好的朋友。在加入罗宾汉之前，他的本名叫做约翰·利特尔，是英国国内最强壮、最高大的人。与其他人不同，他不效忠于任何人，无论是贵族们还是反叛者。他是个勇敢的斗士，独处时才感觉最安全。罗宾汉第一次见到约翰的时候，约翰正在林子旁边的过河小桥上走。桥很窄，只能容一人通过。他们见面的时候，罗宾汉在桥的一头，约翰在

---

lawful *adj.* 合法的
outlaw *n.* 草莽英雄；绿林好汉

right-hand man 得力助手
stroll *v.* 漫步

onto a narrow bridge across a stream. The bridge was so narrow that only one person could cross it at a time. As it happened, Robin Hood *stepped* on it from one side just as John Little stepped on it from the other.

"Step back off the bridge, and let the better man cross first," called Robin Hood. Robin Hood did not think that he was the better man, but he wanted to see what the tall man would do. He had never seen a man who looked so large and strong, yet so *agile* and *skillful*. Robin knew he wanted the stranger to join his band.

"Stand back yourself, for I am the better man," cried the stranger. He had never met anyone who could match his strength and skill.

"Then we have no choice but to fight for it and see who really is the better man," said Robin Hood, who loved a good fight better

桥的另一头。

"退下桥去，谁更有本领谁先过桥，"罗宾汉喊道。罗宾汉并不觉得自己会更有本领，但他想看看那个高个子什么反应。他还从没见过这么高大、强壮的人，而且还这么身手矫健。罗宾希望这个陌生人可以加入他们的队伍。

"我才更有本领，你自己退下去吧，"陌生人也喊道。他还从没碰到过能和他一较高下的人呢。

"那咱们就得过过招了，看看到底谁更有本领，"罗宾汉说。他宁愿少吃一顿饭，也不想错过一场势均力敌的较量。

step *v.* 踏
skillful *adj.* 灵巧的

agile *adj.* 敏捷的

than his dinner.

"With all my heart," answered the stranger with a *grin*.

The Fight

Robin Hood cut two great oak branches to serve as weapons, since it would be unfair to use his bow and arrows when the stranger didn't have any. "The one who can knock the other off the bridge and into the water is the better man," said Robin. They met as eagerly as two young boys wrestling around for fun. The fight with the *poles* began.

What a great fight it was! They struck each other again and again with their heavy sticks. But each man was so strong and skillful in *dodging* blows that neither could knock the other down. Each one got hit many times, until there were plenty of sore bones and *bumps* and

---

"愿意奉陪，"陌生人笑着说。

一较高下

罗宾汉削了两只老橡树枝当作武器，因为陌生人没有弓箭，他用弓箭的话会有失公平。"谁能把对方打下桥掉进河里，谁就更有本领，"罗宾说。于是两个人就像是两个孩子一样迫不及待地扭打到一起。双方的棍棒短兵相接，较量开始。

比试太激烈了！他们手中的重棍一下下地打在对方身上。但是两人都很强劲、灵巧，谁也不能把对方打下桥去。两人也都被对方打得不轻，直

---

grin *n.* 露齿而笑

dodge *v.* 躲闪

pole *n.* 杆

bump *n.* 碰撞

black and blue marks on both their bodies. But neither man thought of stopping for such small things. For a whole hour they fought there on the bridge. Neither one could knock the other off into the water. Then they fought for another hour.

The *smacking* and *grunting* of the battle drew all of Robin's men to the edge of the stream to watch. Some yelled loyally when their leader struck a good *blow* or made a clever dodge. Others, impressed with the *agility* of the stranger, cheered when he landed a blow or whipped his great bulk around so gracefully. They had never seen a man give their leader such a fight.

打得两人全身都是青一块紫一块，骨肉酸痛。但是谁也不会为这点小伤退出打斗。他们在桥上比试了一个小时，但谁也没有把对方打到河里。时间又过去了一小时。

他们的打斗声和低吼声吸引了罗宾的手下们都到河边来观战。每当看到罗宾的精彩一击或迅捷闪躲，就有人衷心地为他叫好；也有些人看到这位陌生人身手敏捷，出手不凡，为他加油，觉得他连辗转腾挪都十分优雅。这些人还没见到谁可以和他们的首领打成平手。

---

smacking *n.* 响声
blow *n.* 一击

grunting *n.* 咕哝声
agility *n.* 灵活敏捷

At last, Robin gave the stranger a terrible *whack* that made him *stagger* and *flail*. But the stranger recovered, and gave Robin a crack on the head that made the blood flow. Robin swung back savagely, but the stranger avoided the blow. The blood ran into Robin's eyes and he could not see, and the stranger gave Robin a smack in the side that tumbled him right into the water.

He lay there looking up and laughing out loud, since Robin Hood never carried a grudge. "You are an expert with that pole; I have never been beaten before," he laughed.

But Robin Hood's followers took it less lightly. Even those who had cheered for the stranger suddenly stepped from behind the trees

---

最后，罗宾重重地打到了对方，那个陌生人没站稳，手臂顺势一挥。但他很快稳住重心，回打到罗宾头上，罗宾鲜血直流。他发疯似的挥舞手臂，但陌生大汉躲开了这一击。鲜血流进罗宾的眼睛里，他看不清东西，陌生大汉这时从侧面重重地打了一下，罗宾跌落到河里。

罗宾脸朝上地躺着，放声大笑，他从来都不会记恨别人。"你真是用棍的行家，这还是我第一次吃败仗，"他大笑着说。

但是罗宾汉的随从们可没这么轻松。刚才还在给陌生大汉加油的人也从树后走了出来，用他们的弓箭对准陌生大汉，不满他把首领击落水中。

---

whack *n.* 重击　　　　　　　　　　　　stagger *n.* 摇晃
flail *v.* （四肢）拼命乱动

with their bows aimed at the man who had knocked their leader into the water. There were nearly forty men, all dressed cleverly in green so that they were utterly invisible behind the bushes. Even with all their yelling, the stranger had not noticed them while he had been concentrating on the fight.

"What has happened, master?" said one of his men. "You are all *bruised* and wet to the skin, and we have never seen you beaten before. Is this some kind of trick?"

"No, no trick at all; this *sturdy* fellow gave me a *walloping* and I tumbled into the water," Robin Hood said.

"Then he shall get a *dunking* and a beating himself," said Will Scarlet. He angrily came forward followed by half a dozen men eager to carry out his threat. But Robin Hood ordered his men back.

罗宾汉一伙有40人，各个身着绿装，就为了方便在丛林中隐藏踪迹。而这位陌生人刚才全心打斗，根本没注意到这群人和他们的喝彩声。

　　"主人，你怎么样？"一个手下问道。"你全身都有瘀伤，满是鲜血，你以前可从没这样过。他是不是耍了诡计？"

　　"不，没什么诡计；这位壮汉给了我一下，我跌进河里了，"罗宾汉说。

　　"那他就应该到水里去泡一泡，再挨顿打，"威尔·斯卡利特说。他带着五六位弟兄怒气冲冲地来到大汉面前，想要吓吓他。但他们被罗宾汉喝退了。

---

bruise *v.* 碰伤
walloping *n.* 重击

sturdy *adj.* 健壮的
dunk *v.* 浸泡

"No," he said, "it was a fair fight, and he won. He is brave and *hearty*, and I would like to have him in our band. Will you join up with us?" he asked the confused stranger. "I am Robin Hood, and my band is the finest in all of England. We steal from the rich and give back to the poor, so that all will be provided for, and justice will be returned to England."

Most men would have *trembled* at hearing the name "Robin Hood," for the lords always described Robin Hood as a cruel and fierce outlaw. But John Little was afraid of no man.

"Why should I join your band as an *underling* if I am a better fighter than the leader? I have no need for people who cannot do better than I can alone. If there is any man among you who can shoot a bow and arrow more *accurately* than I can, I will join," he said. He was

---

"不准动手，"他说，"比试很公平，就是他赢了。他很英勇，也很健壮。我希望他能加入我们的队伍。你愿意和我们一起吗？"罗宾问那位满脸迷惑的陌生大汉。"我是罗宾汉，我们是英格兰最出色的队伍。我们劫富济贫，这样才能让每个人都过上好日子，英格兰才能重获正义。"

大多数人只要听到"罗宾汉"就会全身发抖了，因为贵族们把他形容成穷凶极恶的叛贼。但是约翰·利特尔可不怕这些。

"要是我比你们首领本领更高，我为什么要加入队伍做他的手下？要是没人能打得过我，我就不会与他为伍。要是你们中间有谁能比我箭术更好，我就加入，"他说。他很自信自己的箭术是最好的。

---

hearty *adj.* 健壮的
underling *n.* 手下

tremble *v.* 发抖
accurately *adv.* 精确地

confident that none of them could.

"Well, you are obviously an *extraordinary* man, but I will try," said Robin.

The Archery Match

Robin Hood sent Will Scarlet to cut a three-inch piece of white bark and tie it to an oak a full eighty yards away. The piece of bark looked like nothing but a tiny *speck* in the distance.

"Now choose any of our bows and arrows to shoot with," Robin said.

The stranger chose the largest and most difficult bow, aimed his arrow carefully, and shot it straight into the center of the white bark. The arrow had flown so straight and powerfully and true, only

---

"好吧，显然你技艺超群，但是我还是想试试，"罗宾说。

箭术比试

罗宾汉让威尔切了三英寸的树皮，绑到足足有80码以外的橡树上。远远看去，那块树皮几乎看不清，只是一个小点而已。

"你选你要用的弓箭吧，"罗宾说。

这位陌生人选择了最大、最不好用的弓，认真地瞄准，射在了树皮靶子的正中心。这一箭射得笔直有力，落在靶子上以后只有箭尾羽毛露在外面。罗宾汉的随从们都惊讶地屏住了呼吸，这么精妙的箭术他们也只在罗

---

extraordinary *adj.* 非凡的   speck *n.* 点

its feathers stuck out beyond the bark. All Robin Hood's followers caught their breath in amazement, for they had only ever seen such shooting from Robin Hood himself.

"That is a fine shot indeed," said Robin Hood heartily. "No one can top that, but perhaps I can shoot one just as well."

Then Robin Hood drew his own *elegant* bow and shot an arrow. It flew so straight and *swiftly* that it struck the stranger's arrow dead-on and *splintered* it into pieces. Robin Hood's band gave a mighty roar, and all who saw the arrow cried out that they had never seen such wonderful shooting before.

"Now, will you join my band?" said Robin Hood with a smile.

The stranger saw that he had met his match, and immediately declared his *allegiance*. "With all my heart," he answered.

宾汉身上见到过。

"这一箭射得太好了，"罗宾汉衷心赞扬道。"没有人能射得更好了，但我可以射出同样精彩的一箭。"

然后罗宾汉就拉开他华丽的弓，射出了一箭。此箭又直又快地飞出，正射在陌生人的箭上，把那只箭从中间劈开了。罗宾汉的手下高声喝彩，所有人都觉得从未见过如此精湛的箭术。

"现在，你愿意加入我们的队伍吗？"罗宾汉微笑着问道。

陌生人看见他箭术与自己不相上下，也立即兑现了自己的承诺。"我非常愿意，"他答道。

---

elegant *adj.* 雅致的
splinter *v.* 使裂开

swiftly *adv.* 迅速地
allegiance *n.* 忠诚

Little John

From the minute John Little saw Robin Hood's skill, he loved and respected Robin as his dearest friend. Since he had never been beaten before, he was very respectful of the man who was skilled enough to finally do so.

"What is your name?" said Will Scarlet, taking out a writing *tablet* as though to sign the stranger up.

"John Little," answered the large man. The band of Merry Men roared with laughter.

"I don't like that name," laughed merry Will, "for it doesn't fully describe how small and *puny* you are! We shall call you Little John."

小约翰

从约翰·利特尔看到罗宾汉的高超技艺之后，就非常爱戴罗宾，将他视为密友。他以前也从未遇到过对手，现在终于有人可以和他较量，这也使他对罗宾心生敬意。

"你叫什么名字？"威尔·斯卡利特问道，拿出写字板要把他的名字写上去。

"约翰·利特尔，"这位大汉答道。"快活人"们发出了震天响的笑声。

"我觉得那名字不够好，"威尔开心地笑着说，"因为没描述出来你有多么'小巧'、'瘦弱'！我们就叫你'小约翰'吧。"

tablet *n.* 刻写板　　　　　　　　　　puny *adj.* 弱小的

And so they had a big *feast* to celebrate Little John's entrance into the group. From that day on, Little John was Robin's right-hand man and second in *command*. No one argued with the choice, as he was clearly the best among them all, next to Robin. He served Robin *faithfully* for many years and loved him better with every year.

于是他们就大摆盛宴，庆祝小约翰加入队伍。从那天起，小约翰就成了罗宾的左膀右臂，是队伍中的二当家的。没有人对此有异议，因为小约翰是除了罗宾以外最有本领的人。他忠诚地跟随罗宾许多年，对罗宾的敬爱与日俱增。

---

feast *n.* 盛宴

faithfully *adv.* 忠实地

command *n.* 指挥权

4

Robin Hood and the King

Introduction

Robin Hood and his Merry Men lived in hiding in Sherwood Forest, because every French lord in the land wanted to hang Robin for highway *robbery*. Even though Robin and his band were outlaws, they only stole from the rich, so they could give money to the poor. Robin thought the *greedy* French lords were the real thieves and outlaws. They were the ones who seized the money and land from the poor in the first place. They had conquered England,

盗侠罗宾汉和国王理查德的故事

引子

宾汉和他的"快活人"同伴们藏身在舍伍德森林里，因为当地的法国贵族们都曾被他们打劫，一心想把他们送上绞刑架。即使罗宾汉一群人有时违反了法律，也是因为他们在劫富济贫。罗宾汉认为那些贪婪的法国贵族们才是真正的盗贼和不法之徒，是他们搜刮了穷人的钱财和土地。他们趁理查德国王亲征出战时，占领并统治了英格兰。但是

robbery *n.* 抢劫

greedy *adj.* 贪婪的

and they ruled the land while kind King Richard was off at war. But the French soon found that the English people hated the cruel lords, while they loved and admired Robin Hood. Even the king himself, when he returned from war, could not help respecting this outlaw who tricked the corrupt rulers.

King Richard

"I wish I could see Robin Hood," said King Richard. "I wish I could see him and his men shoot and wrestle and do all the things that show off their amazing skills. But if they heard that the king was coming, they would think that I only wanted to arrest them. They would *flee* deep into the forest and I would never get a *glimpse* of them."

King Richard spoke kindly, for he loved all sports and those who

---

这些法国人很快发现英格兰人民恨透了那些狠心的贵族们，却非常爱戴罗宾汉。即使当国王出战回来时，他自己也不禁尊重起这个"不法之徒"来，因为他在与腐败的统治者们斗智斗勇。

理查德国王

"我真想见见罗宾汉，"国王说道，"我想见见他和他的手下有多么高超的武艺，看看他们射击、搏斗，什么都想看看。但是如果他们听说国王来了，会认为我是来捉拿他们的，他们就会逃进山林，我就再也见不到他们了。"

理查德国王言辞诚恳，因为他热爱所有的体育运动，也敬佩那些运动

---

flee *v.* 逃跑

glimpse *n.* 一瞥

excelled in them. Robin Hood and his band were well known to be the best archers, wrestlers, and sword fighters in all the land. They spent all their days in the forest practicing these arts.

"I would give a hundred pounds to see Robin Hood and his Merry Men of Greenwood," he said.

"I'll tell you how you can see him," laughed one of the king's trusty *companions*. "Put on the robes of a fat *abbot* and ride through Sherwood Forest with a hundred pounds in your *pouch*. You will be sure he will offer you a feast, to try and steal your money." For this was how Robin Hood lured the wealthy lords into the forest. No greedy *nobleman* could refuse a feast, even if they suspected it was offered by an outlaw.

"I'll do it!" cried King Richard, slapping his knee. "It will be a huge

---

高手。罗宾汉这一群人中有全英最出色的弓箭手、搏击者和剑客，他们整日都在森林里练习这些技能。

"如果能见到罗宾汉和'快活人'绿林好汉们，我愿出100英镑。"他说。

"我有办法能帮您见到他们，"一位可靠的随从笑着说，"您只要穿上修道院院长肥大的长袍，口袋里装满100英镑，骑马穿过舍伍德森林，我保证他会盛情款待您，然后想方设法偷走您的钱。"这就是罗宾汉把有钱的贵族们引到森林里的方法。即使那些贪婪的贵族们怀疑是绿林大盗设下的陷阱，也无法抵挡盛宴的诱惑。

"就这么办！"理查德国王拍着膝盖喊道，"这个玩笑开得太好

---

companion *n.* 同伴，随行者
pouch *n.* 小袋

abbot *n.* 男修道院院长
nobleman *n.* 贵族

joke."

The Feast

So the king and seven of his followers dressed themselves as an abbot and seven *friars*. They rode out along the highway toward Sherwood Forest. Sure enough, Robin Hood and his men took them and brought them to the meeting tree, and there they searched them and took the pouch of gold. But they returned one third of the gold to the king, because it was not their custom to leave any man in need. Robin Hood was pleased with these churchmen because they did not resist or *scold* him. In fact, they seemed happy to be in his company.

"Now we shall give you a feast that will be worth all your money," said Robin Hood.

了！"

盛宴

于是国王打扮成修道院院长的样子，带着7个扮成修道士的随从，他们骑马沿着大路向舍伍德森林走去。果然，罗宾汉和他的手下扣住了他们，并把他们带到了那棵他们常聚会的树下。盗侠们搜查了一遍，搜出了一袋金子。但是他们将金子的三分之一还给了国王，因为他们从不将人置之绝境。罗宾汉很高兴，因为这些修道士没有反抗，也没有破口大骂。事实上，他们似乎很高兴。

"现在你们可以吃大餐了，你们的钱就够吃这顿大餐。"罗宾汉说。

---

friar *n.* 修道士

scold *v.* 责骂

"I have a good appetite for a feast," said the pretend abbot. "But even more, I would like to see the archery and wrestling and all those other things in which I have heard you are so good at."

"You will see the very best we can do," answered Robin, "but, Holy Father, why don't you take off your hood so you can enjoy this sweet evening air?"

"No, I cannot," answered the pretend abbot, "because I and my brothers have vowed not to let our faces be seen during this journey."

"Very well, then," said Robin Hood. "I *interfere* with no man's vows." And he never once thought that he was entertaining the king.

Robin and his men gave a splendid feast of roasted *venison* and *pheasants* and fish and wild *fowl*, all cooked perfectly over the roaring

---

这位假冒的修道院院长说："我很想吃顿大餐。但是我早听说你们技艺出群，我还想看看射箭、摔跤，你们做什么我都想看。"

"我们这就让你大开眼界，"罗宾汉回答，"但是，圣父，你为什么不摘下头罩呢？好好享受一下这美好的夜晚。"

"不，我不能摘。"假院长说，"因为我和弟兄们都发过誓，此行不能让别人看到我们的脸。"

"好吧，"罗宾汉说，"我不干涉任何人的誓言。"他从未想过他现在招待的是国王。

罗宾和他的手下了开始准备起了盛宴。有烤鹿肉、野鸡、鱼肉和飞

---

interfere *v.* 干涉   venison *n.* 鹿肉

pheasant *n.* 野鸡   fowl *n.* 家禽

fire. The King was very impressed with the delicious food the Merry Men seemed to produce out of nothing but the forest. He had no idea that outlaws could be so well fed and happy. After they cleared the dishes, they *arranged* the sports.

The Archery Match

The archery target was a mark that only the best archers could hit, made of a tiny *garland* of leaves and flowers hanging from a *stake* a great distance away.

"Now shoot!" said Robin Hood. "Each of you will have three shots, and anyone who fails to place his arrows within the garland will receive a *punch* to the side of the head as hard as I can give."

"Can anyone hit inside that little garland at such a distance?" asked the king in amazement.

禽肉，火势很旺，各种野味烤得吱吱作响。国王很享受这些丰盛的食物，"快活人"们在森林里就地取材，就可以做出如此美味。他没想到这群"不法之徒"可以吃得如此丰盛，过得如此快乐。大餐用毕，"快活人"们就安排了体育表演。

箭术比赛

箭靶是由树叶和花朵扎成的小花环，套在柱子上，中间画了一个靶心。但是距离很远，只有最出色的弓箭手才可能射中。

"开始射击！"罗宾汉喊道，"每人有3次机会，如果谁的箭连花环都没射进，小心我一拳让你脑袋开花。"

"有人能够在这么远的距离射进花环吗？"国王惊奇地问。

---

arrange *v.* 安排　　　　　　　　　　garland *n.* 花环
stake *n.* 柱子　　　　　　　　　　　punch *n.* 拳打

"Look and see, friend abbot," answered Robin Hood proudly.

First, David of Doncaster shot and *lodged* all three arrows within the garland while the king looked on, astonished. Then Midge, the *miller*'s son, also placed all his arrows inside the garland. These truly were the best archers in all of England, and the King had not yet seen Robin Hood, who was the best of all. Then Wat the *Tinker* drew his bow, but he was unlucky—one of his arrows barely missed the mark.

"Come here and take your punishment," called Robin Hood. The king supposed that, since Wat had missed by so little, he would receive only a tap. Instead, he got a blow that knocked him head over *heels*.

"Ha, ha, ha!" laughed his companions.

"亲爱的院长，你瞧着吧！"罗宾汉自豪地说。

第一个上来的是唐克斯特的大卫。他3次都射进了花环，国王看得目瞪口呆。然后是弥奇——一个磨坊主的儿子，他也全部射进了花环里。这些人真的是全英格兰最出色的弓箭手，但是国王还没有看到王者中的王者——罗宾汉的技艺。接着，修补匠瓦特也拉开弓弩，但是他运气不好，有一支箭有点偏差，没中靶心。

"过来，接受惩罚！"罗宾汉说。国王猜想，由于瓦特只是了差一点，他可能只是被轻轻打一下而已。结果，罗宾汉一拳打得他一头跌倒。

"哈哈哈！"他的同伴都大笑起来。

---

lodge v. 将……射入   miller n. 磨坊主

tinker n. 修补匠   heel n. 脚后跟

"Oh ho!" thought King Richard, "I am glad I am not in this." But he was impressed with the way Robin Hood's men obeyed him. "They are better at following his commands than my servants are at following mine," he thought.

The shooting went on, and most of the men shot their arrows within the garland, but a few missed and received *tremendous* punches.

The last to shoot was Robin Hood. His first shaft struck so hard, it split off a piece of the stake on which the garland was hung. His second lodged a *scant* inch from the first. But the last arrow he shot was not feathered right, and it *swerved* to one side and struck an inch outside the *garland*.

"天哪！"理查德国王想，"幸好我不是他们中的一员。"但是罗宾汉的手下对他如此服从，这使国王感慨良多。"他们对他真是言听计从，我的那些仆人对我都没有这么听话，"他想。

射击一直进行着，大部分人都射中了花环的中心，只有几个人失手，都挨了重重的拳头。

最后一个射击的是罗宾汉。他的第一支箭力道深厚，射中了另一支花环中的另一支箭，并且将箭身一分为二。他的第二支箭几乎与第一支不差毫厘。但是他的最后一箭射偏了。它偏向了一边，射在了花环外一英寸的地方。

---

tremendous *adj.* 巨大的
swerve *v.* 偏离

scant *adj.* 差一点点的
garland *n.* 花环

Then all the company roared with good-natured laughter, for they seldom saw their master miss.

"Go and take your punishment, master," said Midge, the miller's son, "and I hope it will be as rough as Wat's was."

"Well," said Robin Hood, "I will *surrender* my arrow to our guest and take my punishment from him."

Robin was being somewhat *crafty* in this. Although he did not mind hard knocks at all, he did not like the thought of being sent *sprawling* in front of his band. He figured that the arms of a churchman would be soft, for they never worked or used their muscles much. But the pretend abbot bared an arm so thick and *muscular* that it made the men stare. King Richard was an active

---

这下所有的同伴们都善意地大笑起来，因为他们从没见首领失过手。

"去吧，主人，去接受惩罚！"磨坊主的儿子弥奇说，"我希望你被揍得像瓦特一样惨。"

"好吧，"罗宾汉说，"我会把我的箭交给我的客人，让他来惩罚我。"

罗宾汉在这一点上有点狡猾，他并不在乎被打，但他不想在手下面前被打得满地找牙。他想，修道士们很少锻炼肌肉，他们的手臂应该没什么力气。但是这位假院长露出了强壮的臂膀，令在场的人瞠目结舌。理查德国王是一个好动的国王，连年征战使他力大无穷。罗宾汉在国王面前站

---

surrender *v.* 交出
sprawl *v.* 笨拙地爬行

crafty *adj.* 狡猾的
muscular *adj.* 健壮的

king, and years at war had made him incredibly strong. Robin Hood placed himself *squarely* in front of him, and the king struck a blow that would have knocked out an *ox*. Down went Robin Hood, rolling over and over on the ground while his men shouted with laughter.

"Well," said Robin Hood, sitting up, half dazed, "I did not think that there was an arm in England that could strike such a blow. Who are you, man? I'll bet you are not the churchman you appear to be."

King Richard *Reveals* Himself

King Richard threw back his hood, and Robin knew it was his king. If he had been a disloyal man as well as an outlaw, he would have *trembled*. But Robin had always remained loyal to his King. Indeed, he believed that stealing from the French and giving to the English poor was the greatest service he could perform for King

---

好，国王挥起一拳，打得他神志不清。罗宾汉被打得在地上打滚，他的手下大笑不止。

罗宾汉眼冒金星，他从地上坐起身说："我觉得在英格兰没有人可以打出这么重的拳。你到底是谁？我敢肯定你是假扮成修道士的。"

国王显露真身

理查德扔掉了头罩，罗宾汉认出他就是国王。如果他真是一个不法之徒，他可能会害怕地发抖。但是罗宾汉一直对国王忠心不二。实际上，他认为用法国人的钱财去救济英格兰的穷人，才是对国王最好的效忠。罗

---

squarely *adv.* 径直地
reveal *v.* 显露

ox *n.* 公牛
tremble *v.* 颤抖

Richard. Robin Hood had never *knelt* for any lord, but there was no shame in his voice when he knelt before the king.

"Your majesty," he said, "you have no *subjects* in all England who are more loyal than I and my Merry Men. We have done no evil except to the greedy and rich who have *abused* your subjects. We beg your pardon if we have done wrong, and we beg for your protection, as we always serve you faithfully."

Then the king looked down in amazement that an outlaw should speak so well. He was also amazed that Robin Hood hadn't run away in fear of being arrested. He saw that Robin Hood truly was one of his best subjects. King Richard also knew that Robin was the best archer in all England, and he wanted him by his side.

"I will forgive all your law-breaking and order the nobles to leave

---

宾汉从未给任何贵族下跪，但是他此刻在国王面前跪倒，讲起话来并无愧意。

"陛下，"他说，"在英格兰，您再也找不到比我们更忠诚的人了。我们从不做坏事，只是惩恶扬善，劫富济贫。如果刚才冒犯了您，还请您宽恕，我们对您忠心耿耿，希望日后能得到您的庇护。"

一位绿林首领如此谈吐不凡，这着实让国王大吃一惊。罗宾汉没有畏捕潜逃，也让国王刮目相看。国王明白，罗宾汉确实是一个好子民。他也知道罗宾汉是全英最优秀的弓箭手，所以他希望罗宾汉能侍奉左右。

"你过去的作为，我既往不咎，我会命令贵族们也不得再纠缠你，"

---

kneel *v.* 下跪
abuse *v.* 虐待

subject *n.* 国民

you alone," he said, "if you will come with me to my court and serve me there. You shall bring Little John and Wat and Will Scarlet to become knights in my court. As for the rest of your men, I will make them royal *rangers*, since I am sure they can protect Sherwood Forest better than anyone. They have done good *deeds* in providing for the English poor."

"With all my heart," replied Robin Hood, and a great roar went up from the Merry Men. They adored their king, and though they loved the outlaw life, they had always wanted their good deeds to be recognized by the throne.

So Robin Hood left the greenwood and went to the king's court where he served King Richard well. His men became rangers of the forest, and never again feared punishment from wicked *sheriffs*.

他说，"但你要到我的皇宫里来，侍奉我左右。你可以带上小约翰、瓦特和威尔，你们都将成为朝廷的骑士。其余人等，我可以赐他们做皇家森林看护员。我相信，他们是保护舍伍德森林的最佳人选。他们已经为英格兰的穷人做了很多善事。"

"遵命！"罗宾汉答道。然后他的同伴们齐声欢呼。他们崇拜国王。他们虽然喜欢不受约束的生活，但也总是希望自己的作为能得到国王的认可。

所以罗宾汉离开了森林，来到皇宫忠心侍奉国王理查德。他原来的手下都成了森林看护员，不用再担心黑心官吏们的惩罚。然而，罗宾汉从未

---

ranger *n.* 森林护林员

sheriff *n.* 官员

deed *n.* 功绩

Robin Hood was never far from the forest, though. He often disguised himself as a greedy noble, *laden* with the king's gold, and rode through Sherwood Forest. Only after his men had stolen from him did he reveal himself, congratulating them on their work. The common folk of England never had to suffer the *injustice* of the French again.

远离过森林。他常常伪装成贪婪的贵族，满载国王的金子，穿越舍伍德森林。只有当那些手下对他行窃时，他才露出真面目，祝贺他们护林有功。英格兰老百姓再也不用忍受法国佬的欺压了。

lade *v.* 装满   injustice *n.* 不公正

5

Makusani's Lesson

This story is based on the character of Makusani, from the creation *myths* of the Yekuana, a small tribe living along the Upper Orinoco River in Venezuela.

The older people tell a story of a boy named Makusani. He was usually a well-behaved boy and always meant to be good. But *somehow* he managed to get himself in trouble without even trying.

马库沙尼的教训

改编自马库沙尼的故事，他是叶库阿纳（委内瑞拉奥里诺科河上游的一个小部落）创世神话中的人物。

老人们讲着男孩马库沙尼的故事。他总是很乖，心地也很善良。可是却总是不知不觉地惹上麻烦。

---

myth *n.* 神话

somehow *adv.* 不知怎么

One morning, Makusani was leaving his house to hunt up in the mountains. His mother told him to be careful and to stay on the *trails*. "I worry about you," she said, as he walked out the door.

"I'll be fine, Mom," he shouted back, carrying his *blowgun* at his side. So Makusani left the village and traveled toward the mountains. There were many small animals to hunt where the forest grew thick.

As Makusani was following the trail up into the mountains, he approached a river. He had passed by this place many times before. But on this day there was a *canoe* tied to the shore. As he walked closer to the canoe, he noticed there was a girl in the boat.

He forgot about hunting and decided he wanted to play with the girl. He *yelled*, "Hi. My name is Makusani. What's yours?"

一天早上马库沙尼正要离开家，去山上打猎。母亲嘱咐他要小心，一定要沿着小路走。母亲在他出门时说："我很担心你。"

"我不会有事的，妈妈。"他背着吹箭筒对母亲喊。就这样，马库沙尼离开了村子，向山上走去。树林深处可以捕到许多小动物。

马库沙尼沿着小路一直走上山，来到了一条小河边。他曾经路过许多次这条小河。但在这一天，他看见岸边拴着一只独木舟。当他走近独木舟时，发现上面坐着一个女孩。

他把打猎的事抛在了脑后，只想着要跟女孩一起玩。他喊道："嗨，我叫马库沙尼。你叫什么名字？"

---

trail *n.* 小径　　　　　　　　　　　blowgun *n.* 吹箭筒
canoe *n.* 独木舟　　　　　　　　　yell *v.* 喊

"Leave me alone," she said. "My father won't let me talk to boys."

"But he won't know," Makusani replied. "Why can't we play?"

She didn't answer. In fact, she ran away.

Makusani thought this was an unusual kind of game, but he followed her. As he chased her, though, she turned into a frog. She *hopped* and hopped, and he couldn't catch her. Makusani ran as swiftly as he could, dropping his blowgun along the way, but she escaped.

He was out of breath. He had *wandered* far from the trail and the rain forest was very thick. He was unsure of how to find his way back to his village.

Makusani sat on a log and thought, "What should I do now? How am I going to get back home?"

"别管我，"她说。"爸爸不让我跟男孩子讲话。"

"他又不在这儿。"马库沙尼回答说，"我们干吗不一起玩呢？"

她没有回答。而是跑开了。

马库沙尼觉得有点奇怪，但还是跟在她后面。可追着追着，女孩变成了一只青蛙。她一蹦一跳的，马库沙尼追不上她。他拼命地追，连吹箭筒都掉在了地上，可还是没追上。

马库沙尼累得气喘吁吁。这时，他才发现自己已经远远地离开了小路，周围都是茂密的雨林。他不知道怎么才能找到回村的路。

他只好坐在圆木上想着："现在怎么办啊？我要怎么回家呀？"

---

hop *v.* 跳

wander *v.* 离开

As he sat there, another girl walked out of a *grove* of tropical trees. "What are you doing here, so far from your village?" she asked. She was a few years older than Makusani.

"I'm lost," he said. "I was chasing a frog, but she got away. Now I don't know how to get back home."

"My name is Huenna," she said.

"I am Makusani," he replied.

"We'll go to my father's house," Huenna said. "He'll know how to get you home." She liked Makusani. He appeared to be a nice boy.

The two went walking off into the forest. After they had traveled for a long time, Huenna stopped to rest.

"I'm *weary*," she said. "Let's rest here for a while. I want to take a quick nap. You stand guard, and don't play any childish tricks on me

---

　　坐着坐着，从一片热带树林中走出一位女孩。"你在离村子这么远的地方干什么呢？"她问道。她只比马库沙尼大几岁。

　　"我迷路了，"他说，"我在追青蛙，可她跑掉了。现在我不知道怎么才能回家。"

　　"我叫胡安娜。"她说。

　　"我是马库沙尼。"他回答。

　　"我带你去找我爸爸，"胡安娜说，"他知道怎么带你回家。"她喜欢马库沙尼，他看起来像个好男孩。

　　他们俩出发向森林里走去。一直走了很久，胡安娜停下来休息。

　　"我累了，"她说，"我们在这里休息一会儿吧。我想打个盹儿。你

---

grove *n.* 树丛　　　　　　　　　　　　　　　weary *adj.* 疲劳的

while I am asleep."

"Okay," Makusani said, wondering how long she wanted to rest.

But after only a few minutes, Makusani was *restless*. Huenna appeared to be asleep already. He dug around under a fallen tree and found a little green *beetle*. He thought it would be funny to put the bug on her arm while she slept.

As he quietly laid the beetle on her arm, she woke up. "I told you not to play any tricks on me," Huenna said. She was very angry. While Makusani was trying to explain that he was only playing, she turned into a tinamou bird and flew away.

Makusani was alone again. He was even more lost than before. He thought, "How am I going to find the trail? How am I going to get

站岗，我睡觉时，不要玩任何幼稚的把戏捉弄我。"

"好的。"马库沙尼边回答边想着她会休息多久呢。

但仅仅过了几分钟，马库沙尼就不安分了。胡安娜看起来好像已经睡熟了。于是他在一棵倒在地上的树下四处挖了挖，找到了一只绿色的小甲虫。他想，要是把这只甲虫放在睡着了的胡安娜身上，一定会很有趣。

他蹑手蹑脚地把甲虫放在了她的手臂上，胡安娜一下子醒了，说："我告诉过你不要捉弄我。"她很生气，变成一只鸟飞走了。马库沙尼还没来得及向她解释自己只是想开个玩笑。

马库沙尼又是一个人了。他甚至比以前更迷路了。他想："我如何才能找到那条小路呢？我要怎么回到家呢？"

restless *adj.* 不安的　　　　　　　　　　　　　　beetle *n.* 甲虫

home?"

He decided to walk down the hill, hoping to find a trail. After walking for a while, he found another river. There was a canoe floating by on the current.

"I'm lost," yelled Makusani to the man in the canoe. "I want to go home."

"Get in," the man said, *steering* the canoe to the edge of the river. "My name is Nanudi."

"I am Makusani," the boy said.

As they floated down the river, Nanudi told Makusani not to open the bag in the bottom of the canoe. Makusani agreed he wouldn't. But the bag was *wiggling*. Makusani was curious about what might be inside.

他决定朝山下走，希望能找到路。不一会儿，他看到了另外一条河。河面上漂着一只独木舟。

"我迷路了，"马库沙尼朝那个独木舟上的人大声喊，"我想回家。"

"上船吧。"那人说着把独木舟划到了河边。"我叫纳奴迪。"

"我是马库沙尼。"男孩儿说道。

他们沿着河向下游划的时候，纳奴迪告诉马库沙尼不要打开独木舟里的袋子。马库沙尼答应了。可他发现袋子在动，很想知道里面是什么。

---

steer *v.* 驾驶

wiggle *v.* 扭动

They came to a rapid where the river was swift. Nanudi had to paddle hard to control the canoe. Makusani thought he could sneak a quick peek inside the bag while Nanudi wasn't looking. When he opened the bag, a *boa* constrictor *uncoiled* from the bag and tried to wrap itself around Makusani.

"I told you not to open the bag," Nanudi yelled as he threw the giant snake into the water. He was very angry. Just as Makusani was trying to explain that he was only being curious, Nanudi turned into an *otter* and swam away.

Without warning, Makusani had to *paddle* the canoe. He didn't know how, so he just steered toward the riverbank. He was relieved when he hit the riverbank.

Makusani pulled the canoe out of the water and started walking downhill. It was getting late now, and he was feeling worried. He still didn't know where he was.

他们划到了一个水流湍急的转弯处。纳奴迪不得不使劲划,才能控制住独木舟。马库沙尼想,他可以趁纳奴迪不注意,偷偷地看一眼里面。他刚打开袋子,一条蟒蛇从袋子里窜了出来,缠在了马库沙尼的身上。

"我告诉过你不要打开袋子。"纳奴迪吼道,他说着把巨蛇扔到了水里。他很生气。正当马库沙尼想向他解释,自己只是好奇的时候,纳奴迪变成一只水獭,游走了。

没有给他留下任何话,马库沙尼只好自己划独木舟。他不会划,所以就只能划向河岸。一靠到岸上,他就长长地松了口气。

马库沙尼把独木舟拉上岸,然后自己向山下走去。天色将晚,他开始担心了。他还是找不到方向。

---

boa *n.* 大蟒蛇　　　　　　　　　　　　uncoil *v.* 解开
otter *n.* 水獭　　　　　　　　　　　　paddle *v.* 用桨划

Makusani climbed up into a tree to rest for a while. He was getting hungry and he didn't even have his blowgun anymore. He had dropped it when he was chasing the frog. As he sat in the tree, wondering what to do next, the boa constrictor *slithered* up the tree. Makusani was afraid, but he was too high to jump.

Suddenly, the snake turned into a girl. She spoke to Makusani: "I am the daughter of the Sun. Because you released me, I will assist you in getting home."

"Thank you," Makusani said, relieved he wasn't going to be eaten.

"There is one condition, though," the Sun Girl replied. "You must always think about how your actions will affect others."

"Is that all?" Makusani *inquired*, relieved this time that he wouldn't have to do anything difficult.

马库沙尼爬上树，休息了一会儿。他越来越饿了，吹箭筒也没了。他追赶青蛙时，弄丢了。正坐在树上想办法时，那条大蟒蛇爬上了树。马库沙尼很害怕，但他坐得太高了，没法往下跳。

突然，那条大蟒蛇变成了一个女孩，对马库沙尼说："我是太阳的女儿。因为你放了我，所以我要帮你回家。"

"谢谢。"马库沙尼松了口气说。这下，他不会被吃掉了。

"但有一个条件，"太阳公主接着说，"你必须要顾及自己的行为会给别人带来什么样的影响。"

"就这个？"马库沙尼问。随即放下了心，好在他不用做什么难事。

---

slither *v.* 蜿蜒地滑动

inquire *v.* 询问

"It's very important," she said. "Your mother has been worried sick about you all day. It's almost nightfall, and she expected you to return home hours ago. Instead, you were getting yourself lost."

"I promise," replied Makusani. He felt bad that his mother had been worried all day. He also felt bad that he put a beetle on Huenna's arm and made her angry.

So, the Sun Girl walked Makusani back to his village. His mother was excited to see him and thanked the Sun Girl *repeatedly*. Just as Makusani's mother was about to invite the Sun Girl to stay for dinner, she turned back into a boa constrictor and slithered into the forest.

"这事非常重要，"她说，"你妈妈肯定一整天都在担心你。现在都是黄昏了，她好几个小时前就在期盼你回家了。而你却使自己迷了路。"

"我答应你。"马库沙尼回答。想到妈妈一整天都在为自己担心，他心里很不好受。想到他把甲虫放在胡安娜手臂上，惹她生气，马库沙尼也觉得不好受。

于是，太阳公主领着马库沙尼走回了村子。妈妈见到他很高兴，不断地说着感谢太阳公主的话。就在马库沙尼的妈妈想邀请太阳公主留下来吃晚餐时，她变回了蟒蛇，滑进了森林。

---

repeatedly *adv.* 不断地

6

The Golden Flute

This story is a retelling of a *folktale* of the Yao people. The Yao live in the mountainous regions of southern China, and also in *Vietnam* and *Laos*.

Once upon a time a woman and her daughter lived in the mountains. The daughter liked to dress in red. For this reason, she was called Little Red.

One day Little Red and her mother were working in the fields. All of a sudden a *gale* blew up, and in the sky there appeared an evil

---

黄金长笛

改编自瑶族民间故事。瑶族人生活在越南、老挝还有中国南部的山区。

很久以前，山里住着一个女人和她的女儿。女儿喜欢穿红色的衣服，所以人们都叫她小红。

有一天，小红和母亲正在田里工作。突然刮起一阵大风，天上出现一

---

folktale *n.* 民间故事
Laos *n.* 老挝

Vietnam *n.* 越南
gale *n.* 强风

dragon. It stretched down its claws, caught Little Red in a tight *grip*, and flew off with her toward the west.

Little Red's mother *vaguely* heard her daughter's words carried on the wind:

"Oh mother, oh mother, as dear as can be! My brother, my brother will rescue me!"

Wiping away her tears, Little Red's mother gazed into the sky and said, "But I only have a daughter. Who can this brother be?"

Little Red's mother *staggered* toward home, and when she had gotten halfway there, her hair caught in the branches of a *bayberry* tree growing by the roadside. While she was untangling her hair, she spotted a red, red berry dangling from a twig. She picked it and swallowed it without thinking.

条恶龙。它伸出爪子，把小红牢牢地抓在手中，向西面飞走了。

小红的妈妈只听见了风中传来了女儿模糊不清的声音：

"哦，妈妈，最最亲爱的妈妈！我弟弟，我弟弟能救我！"

擦干眼泪，小红的妈妈凝望着天空，说："可我只有一个女儿呀。小红哪里有弟弟啊？"

小红的妈妈跌跌撞撞地朝家走。半路上，她的头发刮到了路边的杨梅树枝上。解开头发时，她看到树枝上挂着一颗红色的杨梅。她想也没想就把它摘下来，放进了嘴里。

---

grip *n.* 紧握
stagger *v.* 蹒跚而行

vaguely *adv.* 含糊地
bayberry *n.* 野梅子

When she arrived home, the woman gave birth to a boy with a round head and red cheeks. She named the boy Little Bayberry.

Bayberry grew up very quickly, and in a few days he was a young boy of fourteen or fifteen.

His mother wanted to ask Bayberry to rescue his sister, but she couldn't bring herself to give him such a dangerous job. All she could do was weep to herself in secret.

One day a crow landed on the roof of the woman's house and cried:

"Your sister is suffering out there, out there!

She's weeping in the evil dragon's *lair*!

Bloodstains on her back,

She's digging rocks with hands so bare!"

回到家时，她生下了一个男孩，长着圆圆的脑袋，红色的脸颊。她给孩子起名叫小杨梅。

小杨梅长得很快，几天就长成了一个十四五岁的男孩。

妈妈想让他去救姐姐，可是却舍不得让他做这么危险的事。她只能暗自落泪。

一天，一只乌鸦落在女人的屋顶上叫道：

"你姐姐正在那里受罪，在那里！

她在恶龙的洞穴哭泣！

她的背上都是斑斑血迹，

她在用自己的双手挖岩石！"

---

lair *n.* 兽穴   bloodstain *n.* 血迹

Upon hearing this, Bayberry asked his mother, "Do I have a sister?"

Tears streaming down her cheeks, his mother replied, "Yes, my son, you do. Because she loved to dress in red, she was called Little Red. An evil dragon that has killed so many people came and took her away."

Bayberry picked up a big stick and said, "I'm going to rescue Little Red and kill that evil dragon. Then it can't do any more harm!"

His mother *leaned* against the *doorframe* and through *misty* eyes watched her son march away.

Bayberry walked for miles and miles. On a mountain road ahead of him, he saw a large rock blocking the way that was pointed and rubbed smooth by all the travelers who had had to climb it. One wrong step would mean a *nasty* fall.

听到这，杨梅问妈妈："我有姐姐吗？"

眼泪顺着母亲的脸颊往下淌，母亲回答："是的，我的儿子，你有姐姐。因为她爱穿红衣服，所以她叫小红。有一天，害人精恶龙来了，把她带走了。"

杨梅拿起一根大棍子说："我要救出小红，杀死那条恶龙，它就不能再作恶了。"

母亲倚在门边，泪眼蒙眬地看着自己的儿子走远了。

杨梅走啊走，来到了一条山路前。一块尖锐的巨石挡在了他面前，这块巨石已经被无数翻过它的路人磨得滑溜溜的了。一不小心，就会失足跌到山下。

---

lean *v.* 倚　　　　　　　　　　　doorframe *n.* 门框
misty *adj.* 泪水迷蒙的　　　　　　nasty *adj.* 恶劣的

Bayberry said, "This is my first obstacle! If I don't remove it now, it will be the undoing of many more people." He *thrust* his stick under the rock and *heaved* with all his *might*. There was a great "crack!" and the stick broke in two. Then he put both his hands under the rock and tried to move it with all his strength. The rock rolled down into the valley.

Just at that moment, a shining golden flute appeared in the hole where the rock had been. Bayberry picked it up and blew on it. It gave out a sweet sound.

Suddenly, all the earthworms, frogs, and *lizards* by the roadside began to dance. The quicker the tune, the faster the creatures danced. As soon as the music finished, they stopped dancing. Bayberry had an idea: "Ah! Now I can deal with the evil dragon."

　　杨梅想："这是我遇到的第一个障碍。如果我不把巨石移开,它就会阻碍许多人的行程。"他把木棍插到岩石下面,使出全身的力气向上抬。只听"咔嚓"一声,木棍断成了两半。然后,他又把双手放在岩石底下,拼命挪动石头,岩石终于滚落到了山谷中。

　　就在这时,岩石挡着的山洞里出现了一只金光闪闪的长笛。杨梅拿起长笛,放在嘴边,吹奏出了优美的乐曲。

　　霎时间,路边所有的蚯蚓,青蛙和蜥蜴都随着音乐跳起了舞蹈。节奏越快,它们跳得就越快。音乐一停,动物们就都停止了舞蹈。杨梅灵机一动:"太好了!我有办法对付恶龙了。"

---

thrust *v.* 插　　　　　　　　　　　　　heave *v.* 用力举起
might *n.* 力量　　　　　　　　　　　　lizard *n.* 蜥蜴

80

He strode away with the golden flute in hand. He climbed a huge, rocky mountain and saw a *ferocious*-looking dragon at the entrance to a cave. Piles of human bones lay all around it. He also saw a girl in red *chiseling* away at the cave. Tears were streaming down her cheeks.

The evil dragon whipped the girl on the back with its tail and shouted angrily at her:

"Most ungrateful, *loathsome* Mistress Red!

Since with me you will not wed,

Day by day,

Rock by rock,

Carve me out a handsome cave,

Or I'll send you to your grave!"

他手里拿着黄金长笛，艰难跋涉。爬上了一座巨大的岩石山，在洞口他看到了凶恶的龙，它身边堆满了人骨。他还看到一个穿红衣服的女孩在凿洞，脸颊上流淌着泪水。

恶龙用尾巴抽打着女孩的背，向她怒吼着：

"最忘恩负义的讨厌鬼红！

你永远摆脱不了我。

日复一日地，

一块一块地搬走这些石头，

给我修建一个漂亮的洞穴，

否则我就把你杀掉！"

---

ferocious *adj.* 凶残的   chisel *v.* 凿

loathsome *adj.* 讨厌的

Bayberry realized that the girl was none other than his sister. He shouted:

"Wicked monster! Evil fiend!

To torment my sister so!

Till your *wretched* life shall end,

On this flute I'll blow and blow!"

Bayberry began to blow on his golden flute. The music made the evil dragon dance *despite* itself. Little Red put down her *chisel* and stepped out of the cave to watch.

Bayberry continued to blow on the flute. The evil dragon continued to dance, twisting and *squirming*. The quicker the tune, the faster the evil dragon danced.

杨梅意识到女孩不是别人，正是姐姐。他喊道：

"邪恶的怪物！邪恶的恶魔！

让你折磨我姐姐！

我会一直吹长笛，

直到结束你罪恶的生命。"

杨梅开始吹黄金长笛。音乐让恶龙不由自主地跳舞。小红放下凿子，走出洞外观察。

杨梅不断地吹着黄金长笛，恶龙不停地跳舞，扭动着身体。笛子越吹越快，它跳得也越来越快。

---

wretched *adj.* 可鄙的

chisel *n.* 凿子

despite *prep.* 不由自主

squirm *v.* 蠕动

Little Red came over and wanted to speak to her brother. With a gesture of his hand, Bayberry showed her that he could not stop playing the flute. If he did, the evil dragon would eat them both up.

Bayberry kept blowing for all he was worth, and the evil dragon *stretched* his long waist and kept dancing around in time to the music.

Fire came from the evil dragon's eyes, steam from its *nostrils*, and *panting* breath from its mouth. The dragon pleaded:

"Ho-ho-ho! Brother, you're the stronger! Blow no more! Torture me no longer! I'll send her home, If you leave me alone!"

Bayberry had no intention of stopping. As he blew, he walked toward a big pond. The evil dragon followed him to the bank of the pond, squirming and dancing all the way. With a great *splash*, the evil

---

小红走过来，想和弟弟说话。杨梅用手比画了一下，告诉她自己不能停下来。一旦停下来，恶龙就会吃掉他们俩。

杨梅全力以赴地吹着长笛，恶龙和着音乐摆动着腰身在周围舞蹈。

恶龙的眼睛里冒着火，鼻孔里喷出白色的烟雾，嘴里喘着粗气。他恳求道：

"嘿，兄弟，你真厉害！别吹了！饶了我吧！如果你放过我，我就送她回家。"

杨梅根本不打算停下来。他边吹边朝一个大池塘走去。恶龙跟着他，一路扭动着，跳着来到了池塘的岸边。恶龙跌入了池底，激起一大片水花，池塘里的水面升高了好几尺。

---

stretch *v.* 伸展

panting *adj.* 喘气的

nostril *n.* 鼻孔

splash *n.* 水花

dragon fell into the pond, and the water rose several feet.

The evil dragon was *utterly* exhausted. Fire came from its eyes, steam from its nostrils, and panting breath from its mouth. It begged again in a *hoarse* voice:

"Ho-ho-ho! Brother, you're the stronger!

Let me alone and I'll stay in this pond,

And *torture* folk no longer!"

Bayberry replied:

"Wicked *fiend*!

This is my bargain.

Stay at the bottom of this pond,

And never do harm again."

恶龙精疲力竭了。眼睛里冒着火，鼻孔里喷着白色的烟雾，嘴里喘着粗气。他又用嘶哑的声音哀求道：

"嘿！兄弟，你太厉害了！

如果你饶了我，我就待在这个池塘里，

再也不祸害百姓了！"

杨梅回答：

"邪恶的魔鬼！

这就是我的条件。

待在这个池塘里，

再也不许祸害百姓。"

---

utterly *adv.* 完全地
torture *v.* 折磨

hoarse *adj.* 嘶哑的
fiend *n.* 魔鬼

The evil dragon kept nodding its head. As soon as the golden flute stopped blowing, the dragon sank to the bottom of the pond.

Bayberry took hold of his sister's hand and walked happily away.

Not long after Bayberry and Little Red set off, they heard the sound of water splashing in the pond. They looked over their shoulders and saw the evil dragon *emerge* from the pond. It raised its head and flew in their direction, baring its *fangs* and clawing the air.

Little Red cried:

"Go deep when digging a well;

Pull up the roots when *hoeing* a field.

While that dragon is still alive,

To kindly ways he'll never yield."

恶龙不停地点着头。笛声一停，它就钻进了池底。

杨梅拉着姐姐的手，愉快地走了。

杨梅和小红刚刚动身，就听到池塘里传来巨大的水花溅起的声音。他们回过头，看到恶龙从池塘的水中浮起，抬着头，张牙舞爪地向他们的方向飞来。

小红喊：

"打井要往深里打；

斩草要除根。

只要恶龙活着，

它就不会悔改，永远不会屈服。"

---

emerge *v.* 出现

hoe *v.* 锄草

fang *n.* 尖牙

Bayberry rushed back to the pond and began to blow on his flute once more. The evil dragon fell back into the pond and began to dance again, splashing and squirming in the water.

Bayberry stood on the bank of the pond for seven days and nights, blowing a fast tune on his flute. Finally, the evil dragon could move no longer and floated on the surface of the water. Its days had come to an end.

Sister and brother joyfully returned home, dragging the body of the evil dragon along behind them. When their mother saw her two children coming home, her face lit up with happiness.

They peeled the dragon's skin to make a house, took out the dragon's bones to serve as *pillars* and *beams*, and cut off the dragon's horn to make a *plow*. With the dragon's horn they plowed the fields quickly and had no need of oxen. They plowed many fields, sowed lots of grain, and enjoyed a *plentiful* life.

杨梅急忙跑回池塘，又吹起了笛子。恶龙再次跌进水池里，开始跳舞，在水中扭动，溅起了一片片水花。

杨梅在池塘的岸边站了七天七夜，用笛子吹奏着欢快的乐曲。最后，恶龙再也跳不动了，漂在了水面上。一切终于都结束了。

姐弟俩拖着恶龙的尸体，高兴高兴地回到了家。母亲看到他们回来了，脸上洋溢着幸福。

他们剥出龙皮盖房子，取出龙骨做支柱和横梁，切下龙角做成了犁。用龙角做成的犁耕地很快，根本不需要牛。他们耕了许多地，种了许多谷物，过着富足的生活。

---

pillar *n.* 柱

plow *n.* 犁

beam *n.* 横梁

plentiful *adj.* 富足的

Chinzaemon the Silent

This story is an expansion and adaptation of a Japanese folktale.

A very long time ago, there lived an *armorer* named Chinzaemon. His swords were very beautiful and perfectly balanced. He was famous throughout the land for the quality of his work. Even more famous than his swords, however, were his *scabbards*. Swords slipped into them so easily and silently that other armorers began to call him Chinzaemon the Silent.

A very powerful prince heard about Chinzaemon. The prince

沉默的前左卫门

根据日本民间故事改编和扩写。

很久很久以前，有一个叫前左卫门的铸剑师。他铸造的剑很漂亮也很匀称。精湛的铸剑技艺使他在日本享有盛誉。而经由他打造的剑鞘比他铸的剑更出名。宝剑入鞘时顺畅并且悄无声息，为此铸剑师们都开始叫他"默士前左卫门"。

一位非常有势力的王听说了前左卫门，把他召唤到朝中。王敬佩他打

---

armorer *n.* 铸造武器的人　　　　　　　　　　scabbard *n.* 剑鞘

summoned the armorer to his court. The prince admired the work of the famous silent armorer. He wanted Chinzaemon to make weapons for his soldiers and guards.

Chinzaemon was not only a skillful armorer. He was also very funny and clever. He enjoyed playing practical jokes on people. He had been a very funny child in school. Even while serving his *apprentice* time as an armorer, he continued to tell jokes and play *pranks* on people.

Few people knew that Chinzaemon was such a funny man. He only shared his jokes with people he trusted. So when he made the prince laugh and laugh, for the whole three hours of his visit, Chinzaemon was hired as the prince's new armorer. And no one was more surprised than Chinzaemon. "The prince must be a noble man," he thought to himself. "I will trust him and be very loyal."

造剑鞘的高超技术，想让前左卫门为他的士兵和卫士们铸造兵器。

前左卫门不仅是出色的铸剑师，也很聪明风趣。他喜欢跟人开玩笑。上学时，他就很有趣。即使成了铸剑师学徒后，他也仍然继续讲笑话，捉弄人。

很少有人知道，前左卫门这么有趣，他只是与信任的人分享他的玩笑。所以，他拜访王的整整三个小时，王一直被逗得哈哈大笑。他被王任命为新的铸剑师，这一任命让前左卫门万分吃惊。他对自己说："王是个高尚的人，我一定要信任他，并对他忠诚。"

---

summon *v.* 召唤　　　　　　　　　　apprentice *n.* 学徒

prank *n.* 恶作剧

One night Chinzaemon decided he would play a joke on the guards. He knew that some of them fell asleep while they were on duty. He thought it would be humorous to catch them sleeping on the job. They would be very embarrassed. So Chinzaemon waited until it was very late in the night and then quietly left his room. He moved silently through the hallways until he was out on the palace grounds.

Chinzaemon *sneaked* out to the gate where two guards were sleeping. Using very strong glue made from tree sap, he glued their *sandals* to the ground. He was very quiet so that he did not disturb them. He then did the same thing to four other guards who had fallen asleep.

When Chinzaemon was done gluing the guards' sandals to the ground, he told some other guards about his prank. He then told the

---

一天晚上，前左卫门决定戏弄一下卫兵。他知道一些卫兵会在站岗时睡觉，就想，当场捉到他们当班时睡觉一定很好笑。他们会很尴尬。于是前左卫门一直等到深夜，然后悄悄地离开了房间。蹑手蹑脚地穿过了走廊，一直来到了庭院。

前左卫门溜到了门口，当班的两个卫兵在睡觉。他用树液制成的强力胶把卫兵的木屐粘到了地上。他动作很轻，并没有打搅卫兵的睡梦。接着，他又用同样的方法对付了其他四名睡觉的卫兵。

前左卫门粘完了卫兵的木屐后，向其他的卫兵讲了他的恶作剧。然后，他告诉并说服护卫长敲响警钟。警报敌人来袭的洪亮钟声响起来了，

---

sneak v. 偷偷地走   sandal n. 木屐

head guard and persuaded him to sound the alarm. A very loud bell was rung that signaled an *attack*. All the guards came running except the six who were stuck to the ground. They were glued into place. They couldn't unlace their sandals quickly enough to avoid getting caught.

When the prince came out of his palace to see what had happened, he was still in his nightclothes. The head guard informed him of Chinzaemon's prank. Chinzaemon was afraid that the prince might be angry. He hadn't meant for his little joke to make the prince get out of bed.

But the prince was not angry. For a minute he stood silent, and then he began to laugh. He laughed so hard that he had to *bend* over to catch his breath. The other guards laughed as well. They were glad they weren't the ones who had been caught. When the prince

---

除了那六名被粘在地上的卫兵，所有卫兵都跑过来了。他们六个被粘在了地上，没来得及解开木屐，被当场抓到。

王从宫殿里走出来，看看出了什么事的时候，身上还穿着睡衣。护卫长给他讲了前左卫门的恶作剧。前左卫门担心王会生气，他并没想到这个小玩笑会惊动到王。

不过，王并没有生气。他默默地站了一分钟，然后开始大笑。笑弯了腰，笑得喘不过气来。其他的卫兵们也都笑了起来，他们很庆幸被抓到的不是自己。笑完后，王告诉那些被逮到睡觉的卫兵，他们被解职了。同时

---

attack *n.* 攻击   bend *v.* 弯

finished laughing, he told the guards who had been sleeping that they were fired. He also told them they were lucky he did not have them beheaded.

Later that day, the prince summoned Chinzaemon to his *chambers*. "So," the prince began, "you have caused me to fire six worthless guards. Thank you, oh Silent One." The prince smiled so that Chinzaemon would know he wasn't angry.

"You are welcome," Chinzaemon replied. "But I was only meaning to play a joke." He was a little nervous. But he sensed that the prince was truly grateful for what he had done.

"Well, I feel safer now," the prince said. "You may have saved my life. In return, I will *grant* you anything you wish."

Chinzaemon thought about it for a minute. He already had a good

---

也对他们说，他们很幸运没被斩首。

　　当天晚些时候，王把前左卫门召唤到寝宫，开口说道："你帮我开除了六名不称职的卫兵，谢谢你，你可真是悄无声息啊。"

　　"不客气，"前左卫门回答，"可我只是想开个小玩笑。"他有点紧张，但很快就感觉到王是真心感激他做的事。

　　"嗯，我觉得放心多了，"王说，"你也许因此而救了我的命。作为回报，我将恩准你的诉求。"

　　前左卫门想了一会儿。他已经过上了好日子。但随后他就意识到他可

---

chamber *n.* 寝室　　　　　　　　　　　　　　　　　grant *v.* 准予

life. But then he realized he could use this offer to play a big prank on the courtiers of the prince's court. "Well, noble prince, I have one request." He was a bit embarrassed to ask for what he wanted, but he did so anyway. "Allow me, whenever I want, to *sniff* into your ear."

The prince was shocked. "Strange!" he shouted, laughing again. "You could have chosen anything—gold, silver, land. I don't understand your request. But if that is all you request, it is yours."

"You couldn't have given me anything better, noble prince," said Chinzaemon, smiling.

The next week there was a large gathering at the palace. All the prince's ministers came, as did the *courtiers*. And everyone brought their wives and dressed in their finest clothes. Every month the prince accepted visitors, usually on the full moon.

Everyone who came had some request that they wanted the

以借此戏弄一下朝中的那些大臣们。"嗯，高贵的王，我有一个请求。"他有点不好意思说出他的请求，但无论如何还是说了。"请恩准我，随时闻您的耳朵。"

王很震惊。"奇怪的请求！"边笑边大声说道："你本可以选择包括黄金、白银、土地之内的任何物品。我理解不了你的请求，但如果那就是你想要的，我恩准了。"

"这就是我最想要的，高贵的王。"前左卫门微笑着说。

第二周，宫殿里举办了一场大型的聚会。王所有的大臣和官僚都来了。他们都携带着自己的夫人，盛装出席。王通常会在每月的月圆之日接待来访者。

每个到访者都会提出请求，希望获得王的恩准。这是每个宫殿，每

---

sniff *v.* 闻   courtier *n.* 朝臣

prince to grant. This was the tradition in every palace, in every land, all over the Earth. The prince would consider the requests and do his best to satisfy those he felt were worthy.

Chinzaemon ran over and sniffed in the prince's ear. When they saw him, the ministers and courtiers all thought he was *whispering* something about them into the prince's ear. They all were afraid he might whisper something bad about them that would stop the prince from giving them what they wanted.

So, one after another, the ministers and courtiers all began to give Chinzaemon gifts. They thought that if they gave him gifts, Chinzaemon might *recommend* them to the prince. They didn't know he was just sniffing into the prince's ear. Even their wives would give him gifts before talking to the prince. Chinzaemon just smiled and accepted their offerings. He made them no promises that he would

---

个领地，每个国家都有的传统。王会考虑他们的请求，对那些有价值的请求，他会尽可能地满足。

前左卫门跑过去，闻了一下王的耳朵。王公大臣们看到后，都以为他在王的耳边议论他们。他们都很担心前左卫门说坏话，王会不恩准他们的请求。

于是，王公大臣们一个接着一个地都开始给前左卫门送礼。他们以为给他送礼，前左卫门就会向王推荐自己。他们不知道其实前左卫门只是在闻王的耳朵。甚至他们的夫人在晋见王前，都会给前左卫门送礼。前左卫门只是笑着接受礼品，并没有向他们承诺在王面前帮他们说好话。

---

whisper *v.* 耳语   recommend *v.* 推荐

say good things about them to the prince.

And so it happened. Before anyone dared speak to the prince, he or she would see Chinzaemon first and give him an amazing gift. Soon, the simple armorer was a very rich man. He had piles of money, beautiful gold *jewelry*, *jade* statues, and other fine treasures. He had so many things that he didn't know what to do with all of them. In truth, he was now as rich as the prince, but he still lived as he always had.

Then, one day, the prince turned to Chinzaemon and said, "Well, Silent One, aren't you sorry you didn't ask for anything better from me as a reward?" He saw that Chinzaemon's lifestyle had changed very little over the last months. He wished his loyal armorer had asked for money or land.

"My word, noble prince!" Chinzaemon began, "Something better?

于是，事情就这样发展起来了。每个人在向王进言之前，都会先来拜见前左卫门，并送他厚礼。很快，这个小小的铸剑师就变得富有了。他有成堆的钱，耀眼的金银珠宝，玉石雕像和其他珍贵的宝物。他的宝贝多得都没地方放了。事实上，他现在跟王一样得富有，可他仍然过着以前那样简朴的生活。

然后，有一天，王转向他，对他说："喂，沉默的人，当初你没有向我要奖赏，难道你不感到后悔吗？"王看到前左卫门的生活在过去的几个月里没有什么改变。他真希望这位忠诚的铸剑师向他要求的是钱和土地。

"恕我直言，高贵的王！"前左卫门开口说："我得到的是最好的

---

jewelry *n.* 珠宝   jade *n.* 玉

Why, your favor has brought me so much more wealth than I could ever have imagined. It is more than I could ever need." Then he told the prince what was happening.

When the prince heard how Chinzaemon was making such fools out of his ministers and courtiers (and their wives), he laughed and laughed. He laughed so hard that tears ran down his cheeks.

"So much for my loyal advisors," the prince said. "They aren't much use to me. They are all worthless as advisors. I will *dismiss* every last greedy, foolish one of them." He was actually very angry. He had trusted these people, and they all thought they could buy his favor. He thought about *beheading* them all. He decided he would just fire them all and send them away.

奖赏。您的味道为我带来了从未想到过的大量财富。多得花不完。"之后，他把发生的一切都告诉给了王。

当王听到前左卫门是如何愚弄了那些王公大臣及他们的夫人的时候，王开怀大笑。他笑地流出了眼泪。

"这就是我的谏臣们，"王说，"他们对我没有价值，他们都不称职。我要解除每个愚蠢贪婪的大臣的职务。"王其实很生气，他曾信任这些人，而他们却以为可以花钱买到王的青睐。他甚至想杀了他们，最后决定只是解除他们的官职，遣送回乡。

---

dismiss *v.* 免职

behead *v.* 斩首

The prince summoned his advisors one by one. As they entered his chambers, they bowed and *fidgeted* nervously. To each one he revealed what had happened. They all apologized and begged forgiveness. But the prince told them to leave the palace and to not return.

When the prince had finished dismissing his advisors, he made Chinzaemon his only advisor. The only condition was that Chinzaemon must tell the prince if he ever acted like a fool. Chinzaemon agreed and was given a large piece of land for his *loyalty*.

王逐个召见他的谏臣们，他们进到寝宫后，紧张地鞠躬，坐立不安。王揭露了每个大臣的劣行，大臣们纷纷向王道歉，请求宽恕。但是王让他们离开宫殿，再也不要回来。

王解除了所有谏臣的官职后，任命前左卫门为唯一的谏臣。唯一的要求就是让前左卫门在他做傻事时，提醒他。前左卫门接受了任命，并从王那里获得了一大片土地，作为自己忠诚的奖赏。

---

fidget *v.* 慌张　　　　　　　　　　　　　　　loyalty *n.* 忠诚

8

Odysseus and the Bag of Winds

Prologue

Every culture in the world has its own *mythology*. Mythology is a set of stories from a culture's distant past, sometimes based on true events, but often made up of fantastic events and *supernatural* beings. The purpose of mythology is to entertain, teach lessons on how to live, and help explain how the world works. For example, before humans developed scientific explanations for natural events like earthquakes, storms, and *volcanoes*, many ancient

---

奥德修斯与风袋

序言

世界上每种文化都有其独特的神话故事。神话即来自古代的系列故事集，一部分神话基于真实事件改编，但大多数神话由超自然的奇妙事件构成。神话故事的目的是娱乐大众，教会人们如何生活，并解释地球运转的方式。例如，在人类能对地震、风暴、火山喷发等自然灾害事件做出科学的解释之前，很多古老的神话通过人神之间的故事来阐释

---

mythology *n.* 神话
volcano *n.* 火山

supernatural *adj.* 超自然的

myths explained these mysterious events through stories of gods and humans. The ancient Greeks believed that lightning occurred when Zeus, their *supreme* being, was angry and wished to frighten or punish *mortals* on Earth by throwing down *thunderbolts* from high upon Mount Olympus.

In fact, the mythology of the ancient Greeks is probably the best known of all world mythologies. Greek stories of gods, heroes, and monsters have been studied and enjoyed for more than 30 centuries, and they remain as popular today as ever. Many of the stories of Greek mythology are based on the events of a *monumental* ten-year war between the armies of Greece and a powerful city called Troy and its allies, located in what is now the country of Turkey. All of the Greek gods and many of the great Greek heroes took part in this great war, which is believed to have occurred in the 13th or 12th century B.C.

这些神秘的现象。古希腊人认为，当他们的主神宙斯发怒，想要威吓或惩罚世上的凡人时，他会在奥林匹斯山顶投下雷电，世间就会电闪雷鸣。

事实上，古希腊神话可能是世上最广为人知的神话故事。人们研究神话中的众神、英雄、怪物，长达30多个世纪，并且乐在其中。今天，研究者依然大有人在。多数古希腊神话故事的创作灵感来源于一场长达10年的经典之战——发生在希腊军队和强盛城邦特洛伊（今土耳其境内）及其盟军之间。希腊众神和许多英雄人物均出现在此故事中，人们通常认为这场战争发生在约公元前13或12世纪。

---

supreme *adj.* 最高的
thunderbolt *n.* 雷电

mortal *n.* 凡人
monumental *adj.* 不朽的

The poet Homer wrote a famous account of the Trojan War called *The Iliad*, but perhaps his most famous poem of all explores what happened immediately after the war ended. This masterpiece, called *The Odyssey*, followed the adventures of one of the greatest Greek heroes, Odysseus, as he tried to return home following the war with Troy.

It was Odysseus who won the war for the Greeks by using a large wooden horse to trick the Trojans into opening the gates of their city, not knowing that Greek *warriors* lay hidden inside.

Although his war strategy led to victory for the Greeks, Odysseus still had many struggles to *endure* before he would return home to his family. After the war ended, Odysseus and his men began sailing to Ithaca, their island home. What should have been a simple

---

诗人荷马写过一部关于特洛伊战争的鸿篇巨制——《伊利亚特》。但他最著名的诗篇或许是描述战后故事的《奥德赛》。这部传世之作记述了一位最伟大的希腊英雄——奥德修斯的冒险经历，描述了他在特洛伊战争后设法回家的经过。

奥德修斯用一匹巨大的木马设下陷阱，骗得特洛伊人打开了城门，没想到木马内冲出了藏身其中的希腊勇士。希腊军队由此赢得了战争的胜利。

尽管奥德修斯的战略帮希腊人取得了胜利，但他要想回家与家人团聚，还要经历很多考验。战争结束后，奥德修斯和他的同伴们起航前往家

---

warrior *n.* 战士　　　　　　　　　　　　　　　　endure *v.* 忍受

trip became one of the most famous journeys in all of literature. Odysseus's adventures have been read for centuries, and Homer's model of a hero's journey back home has been imitated in story after story, including movies like *Finding Nemo* and *O Brother, Where Art Thou* and adult novels like *Don Quixote*, A *Farewell* to *Arms*, and *Cold Mountain*.

Odysseus's journey home, which took ten years, was filled with adventure after adventure. His fantastic journey began with the tale of Aeolus and the bag of winds.

A Visit with an Old Friend

After victoriously leaving Troy to sail for home, Odysseus and his men stopped to visit Odysseus's friend, Aeolus, god of the winds. Aeolus welcomed the victors. Odysseus and his men, exhausted

乡伊萨卡岛。这段旅程本应非常简单，后来却成了文学作品中最著名的旅程之一。奥德修斯历险记已被传诵了几百年，而荷马作品中典型的英雄返乡冒险故事也被后人反复用于各种作品之中，包括电影《海底总动员》和《逃狱三王》，成人小说《堂吉诃德》《永别了，武器》和《冷山》。

奥德修斯花了十年时间才回到家乡，途中遭遇了重重险阻。而这场奇妙的冒险记要从埃俄罗斯和风袋的故事开始说起。

拜访老朋友

特洛伊战争取胜后，奥德修斯一行人准备启程返乡。出发之前，他们先去拜访他的一个老朋友——风神埃俄罗斯。埃俄罗斯热情欢迎他们凯

farewell *n.* 告别

after the war, feasted and celebrated for a full month with Aeolus. In return for listening to Odysseus tell many stories of the war, Aeolus offered Odysseus a magical gift to speed him on his way home to Ithaca. The god of the winds gathered all of the wild and dangerous winds that might have blown Odysseus off course. He forced these winds into a magical ox-hide bag, *sealing* them with a golden cord. He left out only one wind, a steady west wind, which would speed Odysseus and his men *homeward*.

With much *gratitude*, Odysseus accepted the gift, amazed that such power could be held in his hands. Not trusting his men to understand such a magical gift, Odysseus quietly *stowed* the bag under the captain's seat on his ship, and the men prepared to sail for Ithaca.

旋。战争使这群勇士筋疲力尽，此时他们终于可以和埃俄罗斯尽情欢乐，大吃大喝，众人庆祝了整整一个月。奥德修斯向风神讲述了许多关于这场战争的故事，为了回报这么多精彩的故事，埃俄罗斯赠予奥德修斯一个能加快他回乡步伐的神奇礼物。风神埃俄罗斯将所有可能威胁奥德修斯航行的狂风邪气都收集到一个神奇的牛皮袋子中，并用一条金色的绳索将其密封。只留下了阵阵温和平稳的西风，助他们加速返乡。

奥德修斯感激万分地接受了这份礼物，他不敢相信自己能够拥有如此巨大的力量。奥德修斯并未指望自己的同伴会理解这份神奇礼物的意义，所以他悄悄地将这个风袋藏到了座位下面。大家准备启程，驶向伊萨卡岛。

---

seal *v.* 封上
gratitude *n.* 感恩

homeward *adv.* 回家
stow *v.* 贮藏

Aeolus's Gift

Aeolus's gift worked perfectly at the beginning of their journey. For nine days, Odysseus's ship carved a smooth and steady wake through the blue waters of the Aegean Sea, always heading westward toward Ithaca. With each passing hour, Odysseus grew more anxious to see his home. The war with Troy had lasted ten long years, and during that time Odysseus had never once seen his wife, Penelope, nor his young son.

He was so determined to return home that he refused to *relinquish* the *helm* of his ship to anyone else. For nine days and nights Odysseus stayed at the helm with his eyes peering through the salt *spray* to catch a glimpse of his homeland. His men were a bit *insulted* at Odysseus's lack of trust in them. They were all good sailors. Of

---

埃俄罗斯的礼物

埃俄罗斯的礼物在航行之初非常奏效。九天以来，奥德修斯的船在爱琴海上航迹平稳，船向西直驶伊萨卡岛。时间分秒流逝，奥德修斯越来越迫不及待，想看到故乡。特洛伊之战持续了十年之久，他已有十年未见到妻子佩内洛普和他们的小儿子了。

奥德修斯归心似箭，他坚持要亲自掌舵。奥德修斯连续掌舵九天九夜，他的目光穿过海雾，偶尔能瞥见远方的故乡。他不信任其他船员，这让其他人感觉受到了羞辱，因为他们都是很出色的水手。我们掌舵水平也

---

relinquish *v.* 放弃   helm *n.* 舵柄

spray *n.* 浪花   insult *v.* 侮辱

course we can steer the ship just as well as Odysseus, they often thought to themselves.

They had also noticed the bag tied with the golden cord sitting under Odysseus's seat—the bag that he seemed to be protecting very carefully. But these concerns were not important to the men at the time. Each of them was also anxious to return home after the war. If Odysseus *insisted* on *steering* the boat by himself, let him do it, they said to themselves. It simply meant they each had more time to sleep and dream of home.

Almost Home

"Odysseus! Look!" Odysseus *snapped out of* his daydreaming as one of his men cried out from the bow of the ship. Shading his eyes from the glare, Odysseus peered ahead. A faint *mist* hovered above

---

是和奥德修斯不相上下的，他们常常这样想。

船员们也注意到了奥德修斯长椅下那个系着金色绳索的袋子——看得出，他很在意这个袋子。不过此时，他们并不关心这些事情。结束了多年征战，每个人都急切地渴望重回故土。如果奥德修斯执意掌舵，那就随他去吧，船员们心想。这只不过意味着他们每个人都有更多的休息时间，还可以在梦中回到故乡。

即将登岸

"奥德修斯，快看！"船上的头桨手大叫道，使奥德修斯突然从白日梦中惊醒。海面波光粼粼，他不禁抬手挡着炫目的波光，眼睛凝视着远

---

insist v. 坚持
snap out of 从……中恢复过来

steer v. 掌舵
mist n. 薄雾

the surface of the water, and *scattered* clouds dotted the sky, but sure enough, as he stared more closely, a familiar outline rose on the horizon. It was the *jagged* peaks of Ithaca! Odysseus could recognize the shape of his beloved island anywhere, and his heart leaped up into his throat to see its familiar *curves* and points.

The rest of Odysseus's men saw the same view a few moments later, and the entire ship erupted into cheers and laughter. Men hugged each other and wiped tears of joy from their eyes. After ten long years of separation from family and friends, they would soon be back home—in perhaps only a few more hours.

As the outline of Ithaca became sharper and clearer, Odysseus's spirits soared. He would finally see his wife, Penelope, and his son, Telemachus. Telemachus was an *infant* when Odysseus left for the

---

方。海面薄雾氤氲，天空云朵散布，不过可以肯定的是，当他又靠近了一些，一个熟悉的轮廓从海平面浮现出来。正是伊萨卡岛错落有致的山峰！无论身在何处，奥德修斯都能认出他深爱的家乡；此刻又见到了熟悉的点点滴滴，奥德修斯激动得心都快跳出来了。

不一会儿，其他船员也看到了远处的家乡，所有人都欢呼雀跃。大家互相拥抱，并抹去对方眼中喜悦的泪水。他们在与家人朋友分离十年后，此刻终于要回家了——也许几小时后就可以进家门了。

随着伊萨卡岛的轮廓在视线里逐渐清晰可辨，奥德修斯兴奋不已。他马上就可以见到妻子和儿子了。当他离家参战时，儿子忒勒马科斯还在襁

---

scattered *adj.* 分散的
curve *n.* 弧线

jagged *adj.* 锯齿状的
infant *n.* 婴儿

war.

How Telemachus would have grown in ten years! Would he even recognize his father? As these thoughts entered Odysseus's mind, his *eyelids* grew very heavy. Ithaca is only hours away. We can see it plainly. Surely I can shut my eyes now and leave the steering to the men, Odysseus said to himself as he struggled to stay awake. Turning to his most trusted companion, Odysseus relinquished the helm, *crawled* over to a nearby bench, and immediately fell sound asleep, dreaming of Penelope and his son.

Jealousy and Greed

With Odysseus asleep and Ithaca within sight, the men began talking quietly to themselves. "Look at Odysseus there—so proud that he was unwilling to let his trusted companions steer the ship."

裤之中呢。

十年了，忒勒马科斯长大了吧！他还会认得父亲吗？奥德修斯想着想着，眼皮开始变得沉重。他心里默念着，剩下几个小时就能到达伊萨卡岛了，小岛已经在我们的视野之内了。现在我可以合眼休息一会，让我的船员来掌舵啦。奥德修斯边默念，边努力保持清醒。然后他让他最信任的同伴来掌舵，自己则跌跌撞撞地走到旁边的长凳前，一碰到凳子就睡着了。在梦里，他见到了妻子和儿子。

妒忌与贪婪

伊萨卡岛已渐入眼帘，而奥德修斯此时正熟睡着，船员们便开始悄悄地议论起来。"瞧瞧奥德修斯，真是太高傲了，都不信任我们去掌舵！"

---

eyelid *n.* 眼皮

crawl *v.* 缓慢地移动

"We've fought together for ten years, and he can't even trust us to steer his ship."

"You know, Odysseus is a great soldier, but he did not share with us fairly the gifts won from Troy."

"That's true. With every victory, he always took the lion's share and left us with the rest."

"Yes, and what about this gift from Aeolus? Odysseus told us nothing of Aeolus's treasure as we left his island."

"Look at that bag, tied with a golden cord."

"Yes, why wouldn't Odysseus tell us about this bag?"

"Because he doesn't want to share with us the gifts of Aeolus."

"Exactly! The bag is surely filled with gold and *jewels*. Just look at that golden cord."

"我们并肩作战十多年了，他居然不放心让我们掌舵。"

"奥德修斯作战是很出色，不过他也不该独吞特洛伊的战利品。"

"没错。每次获胜后，他总是得到最多的好处，把剩下的留给我们。"

"嗯。对了，这次埃俄罗斯给的礼物是怎么分的？离开风神的小岛这么久，奥德修斯对那份礼物只字未提。"

"看那个袋子，系着金线的那个！"

"是啊，为什么奥德修斯不告诉我们这个袋子是怎么回事？"

"一定是他想私吞埃俄罗斯的礼物。"

"没错。这个袋子肯定装满了黄金珠宝，连封口的绳子都是金色

---

jewel *n.* 珠宝

"And look how carefully Odysseus protected it from us."

The more the men talked, the angrier they became at Odysseus and the more anxious they became to open the ox-hide bag sitting under the bench. With one last look at Odysseus sleeping soundly on the bench, the men silently nodded to each other and reached for the bag.

But with one *tug* of the golden cord, everything changed. *Raging*, hurricane-force winds exploded from the ox-hide bag. *Bottled* up for the last nine days, winds from every direction *furiously* crashed down and around Odysseus's ship, tossing it around on the waves as if it were a child's toy.

Odysseus's sweet dreams of home turned into a nightmare of howling winds and crashing waves. Opening his eyes, he saw his

---

的。"

"看奥德修斯把它藏得多隐蔽。"

大家越相互吐苦水，就对奥德修斯越不满，也越等不及想打开长凳下面的牛皮袋。他们又看了一眼躺在长凳上熟睡着的奥德修斯，然后互相点头示意，将风袋拿了起来。

但那条金色绳子一解开，一切都变了。狂暴猛烈的风从牛皮袋中呼啸而出。狂风邪气在被困缚了九天之后，从四面八方肆虐而来，船只就像一个玩具般被狂风玩弄，在海面上颠簸不定。

奥德修斯回家的美梦变成了充斥着狂风巨浪的噩梦。他睁开双眼，只

---

tug *n.* 拽
bottle *v.* 抑制；约束

rage *v.* 肆虐
furiously *adv.* 狂暴地

men panicking, rushing around the deck, waving their arms, and covering their heads against the winds and waves. At their feet, he saw the empty ox-hide bag. "What have you done?" he cried. "Your greed and jealousy have ruined us!"

Unable to hear Odysseus over the howling winds, the men rushed over the ship, trying to keep it from *capsizing* in the storm. Suddenly, with a great snapping and *ripping* sound, the mast came *crashing down*, pulling the sails with it.

Heartbroken, Odysseus watched helplessly as his home began *fading away* in the distance. With no sails on the ship and no way to steer, Odysseus and his men were being blown over the furious seas away from Ithaca, back in the direction from which they'd come.

Oh, weak man! Why did I let myself sleep? Odysseus cried to

见船员们一片慌乱，在甲板上站也站不稳，他们挥舞着手臂，还裹着头以躲避风浪的袭击。奥德修斯在他们的脚下看到了一个空空的牛皮袋。"看看你们干的好事！"他大喊道。"你们贪婪、妒忌，把一切都毁了！"

海风咆哮着，船员们听不见奥德修斯在说什么。他们在船上奔忙着，试图保护船只不要在风暴中沉没。突然，随着一阵巨大的撕裂声，桅杆朝下猛撞，而帆布也被连根拔起。

奥德修斯万念俱灰，他无助地望着视野内远去的故乡。船帆已毁，奥德修斯和船员们无法控制航向，只能任狂暴的大海卷着船只离伊萨卡岛愈来愈远，最后竟原路返回到出发地。

真没出息，你怎么能睡着呢？奥德修斯自己大喊道。就剩几个小时就

---

capsize *v.* 倾覆
crash down 倒塌

rip *v.* 撕裂
fade away 消失

himself. Hours from home, and now this! He prayed to Poseidon, god of the seas, to calm the waves, and to Zeus, god of the sky, to end the storm. However, his prayers went unanswered. The gods had other things in store for Odysseus, and he would not see his home for many more years.

Epilogue

Driven by the howling winds, Odysseus and his men *cowered* in fear onboard their ship, helpless to sail in the storm. *Eventually*, they ended up back at Aeolus's island. "Odysseus, why are you here?" Aeolus asked, as the men came ashore.

With great shame, Odysseus told Aeolus what happened with the bag of winds. "It was not my fault," he said. "It was my men." He pleaded with Aeolus to help him once again.

到岸了，现在一切都完了！他祈求海神波塞冬平息海浪，恳求主神宙斯结束这场风暴，可是叫天天不应，叫地地不灵。而众神已经为奥德修斯安排了其他考验，他要在多年后通过考验时才能回到家乡。

后记

海面狂风呼啸，奥德修斯和同伴被困在船上，深感恐惧不安。船只在风暴中无力地飘摇着。最终，他们回到风神埃俄罗斯的岛上。一上岸，埃俄罗斯便问："奥德修斯，你们怎么在这儿？"

奥德修斯觉得很丢脸，但他还是对埃俄罗斯讲了风袋的事情。"不怪我，"他说，"是我手下的船员干的。"他恳求埃俄罗斯能够再帮他一

---

cower *v.* 畏缩   eventually *adv.* 最终

However, despite Odysseus's *desperate* pleadings, Aeolus was firm. "Surely the gods have decided to test you, Odysseus," he said. "To be turned away after getting so close to home can only mean the gods are against you, and I cannot go against the gods' wishes. Good luck to you, wise Odysseus. I cannot help you again."

Aeolus was right. Odysseus would suffer much bad luck, and struggle mightily, before he would finally reach Ithaca. But these journeys proved Odysseus to be the *craftiest*, most clever mortal on Earth, and his journey became one of the greatest stories ever told.

Look for *The Odyssey* at your local library or bookstore. Read about the many adventures of Odysseus and how human traits such as *jealousy*, pride, *gluttony*, and others prevented him and his crew from returning home sooner.

次。

　　然而，尽管奥德修斯苦苦哀求，埃俄罗斯始终无动于衷。"奥德修斯，上帝一定是在考验你，"他说，"离家仅一步之遥时却无功而返，只能意味着上帝在锤炼你，而我万万不能违背上帝的意旨。聪明的奥德修斯，祝你好运吧。我真的不能再帮你了。"

　　埃俄罗斯是对的。在奥德修斯最终到达伊萨卡岛前，他将经历重重险阻，还免不了殊死搏斗。但是，这些历程终将证明奥德修斯是世上最聪明机智的人，而他的旅程也将成为史上佳话之一被人们传诵。

　　到当地的图书馆或书店找找《奥德赛》这本书吧！阅读奥德修斯的历险记，可以了解到人类的天性——如妒忌、傲慢、贪婪等——如何使得奥德修斯和同伴们难以顺利返乡。

---

desperate *adj.* 绝望的
jealousy *n.* 妒忌

crafty *adj.* 狡猾的
gluttony *n.* 贪吃贪喝

9

Miguel and **K**ing Arthur

The King's Diamond

Ninth *inning*. One out. *Bases* loaded.

Miguel Ventura stood at bat. Two strikes. He had to make contact.

Sweat *trickled* down Miguel's face, and his shoulders ached. He called time, and sunlight reflected off the bat, creating a burst of color like a million tiny rainbows. He took a deep breath.

米格尔和亚瑟王

金牌球王

到了第九局，第一棒打偏了，满垒。

米格尔·文图拉手拿球棒站着，第二棒又扑空了，最后一个球他必须击中。

汗水顺着米格尔的脸颊流淌下来，他感到肩膀酸痛。于是他叫了一次暂停，深吸了一口气。阳光映射在球棒上，折射出斑驳的色彩，犹如七色彩虹交织。

---

inning *n.*（棒球或垒球比赛的一）局   base *n.*（棒球等的）垒
trickle *v.* 滴；流

It was time. Now or never.

Back at home plate, Miguel *cranked* the bat up into the air. A fastball sailed toward him. He swung. THUD! The ball hit the catcher's *mitt* as the rival team roared their approval.

Miguel couldn't hide his disappointment as he jogged to the *dugout*. The other team needed one more out to win the game. He had pictured himself hitting the winning home run and his teammates lifting him high into the air after he crossed home plate. The imagined roar of the crowd was ringing in his ears still. He barely noticed Trevon as he walked toward home plate.

Trevon held his bat high like a marvelous sword. The first pitch *hurtled* toward home plate. Trevon swung. SMACK!

Going. Going. Gone! Grand slam!

暂停时间到，胜败在此一举。

回到本垒，米格尔转了转球棒，双手拿稳举在空中。一个快球向他飞来，挥棒，砰！球稳稳落在对方捕手的手套中，对方球员顿时欢呼起来。

他拖着脚步走下场，难掩内心的失望。本队再有一名选手淘汰，对方就赢了。他曾幻想着自己成功全垒打的场景：队友把他抛向空中，阵阵欢呼在耳边荡漾。他还没回过神来，特雷文已经上场了。

只见特雷文把球棒高高举起，就像骑士高举着宝剑。对方发起进攻，向本垒抛出一记快球，特雷文挥棒，啪的一声，击中了！

快跑，快跑，漂亮极了！全垒打！

---

crank *v.* 转动曲柄
dugout *n.* 休息棚

mitt *n.* 棒球手套
hurtle *v.* 飞速移动

"Yes!" Miguel yelled, meeting his friend as he crossed home plate.

Miguel's teammates gathered Trevon up onto their shoulders. The crowd roared, and his family rushed out to meet him. The girls in the front row smiled and waved. Miguel felt a *twinge* of jealousy.

Trevon was the golden boy. His life looked good.

On the way into the pizza parlor, Miguel said, "I need some batting tips, Trevon." He pushed past a brown-haired girl from the front row.

Trevon glanced back, but Miguel *ushered* him on. "I've struck out ten times in the last three games. Coach is going to bench me unless I get some help."

"Ask Leo," Trevon said. "He's got a *decent* batting average."

"太棒啦！"米格尔边喊边向刚刚到达本垒的特雷文冲过去。

队友们把特雷文举过肩膀，观众也开始欢呼雀跃，他的家人也从观众席飞奔过来。坐在前排的女孩们微笑着向特雷文招手，米格尔顿时心生嫉妒。

特雷文一直是金牌球员，他的生活总是顺风顺水。

米格尔在往比萨店里走时说："特雷文，你得教我点击球技巧。"说着话用力从前排的一位棕发美女身边挤了过去。

特雷文不住地往后看那女孩儿，米格尔迎了上去说："我前三场比赛出局十次，你要是不帮帮我，教练会让我坐冷板凳的。"

"你去问里欧好了，他的击球技术很过硬。"特雷文说。

---

twinge *n.* 一阵刺痛
decent *adj.* 相当好的

usher *v.* 迎接

"Not like you," Miguel said. "You're the king." Miguel *grabbed* four slices of pizza off the table. "It's time for the king to share his wealth. Let's meet at the batting cages every day this week."

"Share my wealth?" Trevon said. "If I'm coaching you every day, when am I going to practice?"

"You've got your glory," Miguel said. "Now you can spread it around."

The brown-haired girl waved again. Trevon waved back.

"So, is it a deal?" Miguel asked, thinking that being the star of the team would feel mighty good.

"I've got homework, and I have to babysit my cousin."

"Since when have homework and babysitting come before baseball?"

"他比不上你，你是球王。"米格尔说着从桌上一把抓起四片比萨，"现在球王应该分享些秘诀了，这周我们每天在棒球场碰面好不好。"

"分享秘诀？那我哪有时间练球了？"特雷文说。

"你该得的荣誉也得了，现在也该让我们沾沾光。"米格尔说。

那个棕发美女又向这边招手，特雷文也向她挥手回应。

"那就这么定了？"米格尔问道，心想成为球队明星的感觉一定很不错。

"我要做作业，还得照看我表弟。"

"从什么时候开始，做功课和当保姆比打球更要紧了？"

---

grab *v.* 抓

"He's a star," Leo pointed to the girls smiling at Trevon. "And he wants to stay one."

Miguel *swallowed*. "Is that true?"

Trevon couldn't find the words to explain.

"See?" said Leo. "C'mon, Miguel. We're not royal enough for this table. Kings aren't a part of any team."

The Destiny of the Sword

At Saturday's game, Miguel struck out twice but managed one base hit. Trevon hit two doubles and a triple, and now had a whole fan section in the front row. He seemed not to care that Leo and Miguel hadn't been speaking to him since last week.

"他是大明星嘛，"里欧指着那些对特雷文抛媚眼的女孩们对米格尔说，"他可不想让别人抢了这头衔。"

"是这样吗？"米格尔忍不住问道。

特雷文一时不知道该怎么解释。

"看到了吧！过来吧，米格尔，我们还不够资格跟他用一张桌子。球王是不属于任何一个球队的。"里欧说。

宝剑的宿命

在星期六的比赛中，米格尔两次出局，还好有一次安打。特雷文则是两次二垒安打，一次三垒安打，前排的观众都成了他的粉丝。他似乎都没注意到，从上个星期开始，里欧和米格尔再也没有跟他说过话。

---

swallow *v.* 忍受

"Since when did the three *amigos* become two?" Miguel's sister, Teresa, asked.

Miguel shrugged, placing his bat into his bag and walking toward the field.

"Aren't you coming for pizza?" she asked.

"Nah, I'm going back to the shop."

"To visit *the Great Gallardo's* books?"

"Just go eat pizza, and I'll see you later."

Miguel and Teresa both had become characters in *the Great Gallardo's* magic books they'd found in the *loft*. Leo and Trevon had even traveled inside a book with Miguel once, but Trevon was now probably too busy with his fan club to come along on an adventure.

"什么时候三剑客变成两剑客了？"米格尔的妹妹特丽莎问道。

米格尔耸了耸肩，把球棒放回包里，向球场走去。

"你要不要一起去吃比萨？"妹妹问道。

"不去，我要回去店里。"

"去看《伟大的贾拉多》吗？"

"去吃你的比萨吧，待会儿见。"

自从在阁楼里发现《伟大的贾拉多》系列魔法书，特丽莎和米格尔似乎都化身成为书中的人物。里欧和特雷文也曾与米格尔随着书中的一个故事神游，但现在，特雷文没有时间去读别人的历险故事，他正忙着组织自己的球迷俱乐部呢。

---

amigo *n.* 朋友　　　　　　　　　　　　　　　　　　loft *n.* 阁楼

Up in the loft, a thick purple book waited for Miguel on the *enchanted* chest. "Le Mort d'Arthur," Miguel read. "*The Knights of the Round Table!*"

He opened the book to page 98, and stars appeared in his eyes as he whispered aloud, "I could become King Arthur!"

"WHOSO PULLETH OUT THIS SWORD FROM THE STONE THAT SAME IS RIGHTWISE KING BORN OF ENGLAND," Miguel read, but the words hopped around the page. "gaze at people Many sword *marvel* came on to the and its beauty."

The silence disappeared, and Miguel found himself surrounded by a group of knights, *clanking* swords around his head. He *ducked*, knocking his heavy helmet into another knight.

上了阁楼，一本厚厚的紫色封皮的书摆在书架上等着米格尔。"莫特·亚瑟，《圆桌骑士》！"米格尔读出声来。

他把书翻到98页时，自言自语道："我能成为亚瑟王！"说着这句话时，眼睛开始闪闪发亮。

"谁能把剑从石头里拔出来，谁就是英格兰真正的国王。"米格尔读着，书中文字似乎都在页面上跳起来，变得模糊，"他的眼前出现了很多剑客围在他的身边，他们都啧啧称赞着一把举世无双的宝剑。"

米格尔突然发现周围开始喧嚣，一群骑士正包围着他，手里拿着的剑都对准他的头。他急忙闪躲，结果重重的头盔又狠狠撞到了另一个骑士。

---

enchanted *adj.* 施过魔法的
clank *v.* 发出叮当声

marvel *n.* 令人惊奇的事物
duck *v.* 躲避

"Sir Kay!" the knight roared. "Do you challenge me?"

Miguel shook his head. "No, sir." But his words were lost in loud clash of metal upon metal. His massive *opponent* wore a suit of midnight black armor.

Miguel tried to escape, but the *bulky* armor weighed him down like an elephant on his back. The black knight raised his *humongous* sword high in the air. Out of *instinct*, Miguel lifted his arm, surprised to find that he, too, held a sword. His blade trembled, glistening in the sun as he gripped it with all his might.

"It is time for the great Sir Kay to fall," shouted the black-armored knight.

The words made Miguel's body quake.

"凯伊骑士，你是在向我挑战吗？"那个骑士大喊道。

米格尔摇摇头，"不，先生。"但他的声音被金属撞击声音所吞没。他的对手很强大，是一位身穿黑铠甲的骑士。

米格尔企图逃走，但沉重的铠甲就像一头大象压在他背上。这黑甲骑士正高举起手中的重剑。米格尔出于本能举起胳膊，却惊讶地发现他手中也拿着一把剑。他手中的宝剑在太阳下闪闪发光。他用尽所有的力气紧紧握剑，只见剑锋发抖。

"该是凯伊爵士下台的时候了。"穿着黑甲的骑士高喊道。

这话让米格尔全身一颤。

---

opponent *n.* 对手

humongous *adj.* 巨大无比的

bulky *adj.* 笨重的

instinct *n.* 本能

The knight slashed Miguel's sword, slicing it in half as though it were a blade of grass.

"Sir Kay!" From the crowd, a young man rushed forward.

Miguel stared, dropping what was left of his weapon.

"Shall I fetch you another sword, brother?"

Dazed, Miguel nodded, and off the boy ran.

Miguel's thoughts *churned*. This must have been a *tournament* between the great knights in celebration of the sword in the stone. And if he was Sir Kay, then the young man who ran to get him another sword was...

黑甲骑士挥过来的剑把米格尔的剑劈成两半，米格尔的剑就像玻璃一样不堪一击。

"凯伊爵士！"从人群中突然冲出一个年轻人。

米格尔盯着他，扔下手中破碎的宝剑。

"需不需要我再拿把剑给你，哥哥？"

米格尔还没弄明白是怎么回事，就点了点头，然后那年轻人就跑开了。

米格尔思忖着，这一定是给那些伟大的骑士们举办的比武大赛，就是为了庆祝从石头中拔出宝剑。如果他自己是凯伊爵士的话，那跑来要帮他拿另一把剑的年轻人就是……

---

churn *v.* 搅动

tournament *n.* 比赛

"Arthur!"

"I'm here, brother."

Miguel turned to the young man, who held a beautiful, *glistening* sword.

"Excalibur!"

All Hail the True King of England!

The magnificent sword *electrified* Miguel's hands as he turned to face the black knight once more. Merlin's magic! He felt renewed. Energy coursed through his *veins* as, clang for clang, he met the black knight's blows with Excalibur. Soon the black knight *faltered*;

"亚瑟！"

"我在这，兄弟。"

米格尔转过身，看见那年轻人手上拿着一把闪着金光的宝剑。

"亚瑟王神剑！"

英格兰国王万岁！

当再次面向那个黑甲骑士时，这把神剑赐给了米格尔力量。是梅林的魔法！他感觉自己精神焕发、气血强劲、哗哗作响，他用亚瑟王神剑与黑甲骑士对抗。很快，黑甲骑士就有些招架不住了，米格尔亮剑、挥剑，仿

---

glisten *v.* 闪耀

vein *n.* 血管

electrify *v.* 使通电

falter *v.* 踉跄

Miguel saw his opening and swung Excalibur, connecting with the knight's sword as though it were a baseball and Excalibur were a bat. The black knight's sword flew out of his hands as though Miguel had just hit a *grand slam*.

The crowd roared and clapped its *approval*.

Miguel *grinned* broadly behind the faceplate of his armor helmet. The black knight bowed his head toward Miguel before turning to make sure his squire *retrieved* his sword. Miguel acknowledged the act of respect with a tilt of his head.

Arthur ran up to congratulate his brother.

"My brother, you courageously faced near-defeat as a true nobleman and took victory. I am honored to be your kinsman."

佛手上握着的亚瑟神剑就是球棒，他把黑甲骑士的剑打得脱了手，赢了个大满贯。

人群发出叫好的欢呼声和热烈的掌声。

米格尔暗自庆幸，在头盔面板后笑得嘴都合不拢了。黑甲骑士向米格尔鞠躬，请求米格尔让他拿回自己的剑。米格尔很有礼貌地点了点头，表示默许。

亚瑟跑过去祝贺他哥哥。

"哥哥，你是真正的贵族，真勇敢，即使面对不利的战局，也能取得最后的胜利。我很自豪有你这样的兄弟。"

---

grand slam 大满贯
grin *v.* 露齿笑

approval *n.* 赞许
retrieve *v.* 取回

"As am I," stated Sir Ector, whom Miguel remembered was Sir Kay's father and the man who had raised Arthur as though he were his own son.

"You will be unbeatable in the *joust*, my son."

"But what is this sword?" Sir Ector inquired, shock and *puzzlement* twisting his features.

Miguel knew with certainty it was the sword from the stone—the sword that made whoever could pull it from the stone the king of all England. However, he held his tongue. The glory and *adoration* of being king tempted Miguel. He had tasted Excalibur's power in the *duel*. King Arthur was beloved by all the knights of the Round Table; why then could they not love King Kay just as much?

"我也是，"埃克特爵士说道。米格尔记得他是凯伊爵士的父亲，他把亚瑟当自己亲生儿子一样抚养。

"我的儿子，你会在竞技中所向披靡的。"

"但这是一把什么剑呢？"埃克特爵士问道，心头满是不解和困惑。

米格尔当然知道这是石头上插的那把剑——谁能够把它从石头里拔出来，他便是英格兰真正的国王。但是，他没有说出来。对王权的崇拜和王位的荣耀诱惑着米格尔。他在决斗中已经尝到的亚瑟神剑的神力。圆桌骑士爱戴亚瑟王，为什么他们就不能同样爱戴凯伊王呢？

---

joust *n.* 比武

adoration *n.* 崇敬

puzzlement *n.* 不解

duel *n.* 决斗

"Where did you get the sword?" Sir Ector demanded.

"I brought it to him, Father," said Arthur. "I couldn't find another blade, so I thought of the sword I saw stuck in the stone near the *cathedral*. I pulled on it, and it came out with *marvelous* ease."

Arthur had no idea what he had done.

Miguel felt a twinge of regret deep in his stomach as he faced Arthur, but he *plunged* ahead anyway.

"It was I who pulled the sword from the stone, Father," Miguel lied, knowing deep down the sword did not belong to him. "Arthur just fetched Excalibur for me."

"I do not understand why you dishonor yourself and our father with lies, Kay," Arthur challenged. His feelings about doing what was right *dominated* the loyalty he felt toward Sir Kay.

"你从哪里得来的剑？" 埃克特爵士厉声问道。

"父亲，是我拿给他的，"亚瑟说，"我也不知道在哪里能找到剑，就想起了在教堂附近插在石头里那把，我一下就把它拔了出来，完全没费劲。"

亚瑟当然不知道自己完成了一件多么伟大的事情。

面对亚瑟时，米格尔感到深深地愧疚，但他还是硬着头皮说：

"是我把剑从石头里拔出来的，父亲。"米格尔明明知道这把剑并不属于他，但还是撒了谎，"亚瑟只是帮我把神剑拿过来而已。"

"凯伊，我不知道你为什么要对父亲撒谎，真丢人。"亚瑟反驳道。他对凯伊很忠诚，但他对事实真相更为忠诚。

---

cathedral n. 大教堂
plunge v. 插入

marvelous adj. 不可思议的
dominate v. 控制

"Enough!" roared Sir Ector. "Whichever of you pulled the sword from the stone will be able to repeat the task tomorrow morning. For tonight, we will celebrate Sir Kay's victory in the duel and wish him well in the joust."

Weary from the day's tournament, Sir Ector retired early, and Miguel basked in the *glow* of his admirers as knights celebrated around campfi res that night. Word had *rapidly* spread that he had pulled the sword from the stone and would do so again in the morning. Arthur watched from the edges of the fire's circle, now realizing the importance of the sword and the *swindle* Kay was trying to pull.

The next morning, following a procession of knights, kings, and their royal courts, Miguel went to the stone. The crowd parted,

---

"够了！"埃克特爵士喊道，"不管是你们谁从石头里拔出的剑，明天早上都要再拔一次。今晚，我们先庆祝凯伊在决斗中的胜利，庆祝他在竞技中的优异表现。"

白天的比赛令埃克特爵士很疲倦，他早早就休息了。而米格尔则在接受他的仰慕者的推崇，骑士们一晚上都在篝火旁庆祝。消息很快传开，大家都知道是他拔出的剑，而且明天早上还会再拔一次。亚瑟远远地站在篝火外围，看着他们庆祝，现在他意识到了那把剑的重要性，以及凯伊之前为什么要撒谎。

第二天早上，米格尔也来到那块石头跟前，身后跟随着一群骑士以及

---

glow *n.* 光辉   rapidly *adv.* 迅速地

swindle *n.* 欺诈

leaving a tall, bearded man in its wake. Merlin! As he walked forward, his gray velvet cape dragged behind, leaving *iridescent* swirls in the soil. His eyes were intense, as though Miguel were looking through a microscope into Merlin's soul.

"Sir Kay," Merlin said. "Let us watch the miracle."

Miguel stepped forward, Excalibur *clamped* tightly in his hands, focusing as though he were at home plate, picturing a home run. Maybe he could actually pull the sword from the stone! Before he *tugged* at the blade, someone shouted, "*Intruders*! Beyond the hills!"

The knights mounted their horses, and Arthur pointed them east over the hills. Everyone rushed to battle, leaving Miguel and Arthur alone.

王侯和皇室成员。人群分站在两边，只剩下一个高高的、留着胡子的男人站在中间。是梅林！当他向前迈步时，他灰色的巫师帽掉了下来，在地上打着转，闪闪发光。他目光如炬，好像把米格尔看透了。

"凯伊爵士，让我们见证奇迹的发生吧。"梅林说道。

米格尔走向前，双手握紧亚瑟神剑，脸上的表情就像他站在本垒时一样全神贯注。此时他脑子里想象着来一个满垒跑。也许他真的可以把剑从石头里拔出来！在他正要用尽全力拔剑的时候，突然有人喊道，"有敌人！就在山后面!"

骑士们都飞身上马，亚瑟指向山的东面，他们都向敌人的方向奔去，只剩下凯伊和亚瑟。

---

iridescent *adj.* 彩虹色的

tug *v.* 使劲拉

clamp *v.* 夹住

intruder *n.* 侵入者

"Here," Arthur said, grabbing the sword's hilt, "If you want glory for your *treachery*, take it."

Miguel stared at Arthur and Excalibur.

As though the stone were butter, Arthur slid Excalibur from its home and kneeled down before Sir Kay, just as the crowd returned.

"He's done it!" Arthur said. "Sir Kay is the true King of England!"

Every single person crouched down before Miguel, even Merlin.

"Wait."

Nobody heard him.

"All hail King Kay!"

亚瑟卧着剑柄对他说："好吧，如果你骗人就是为了得到荣耀，就把剑拿走吧。"

米格尔看着亚瑟，又看了看神剑。

眼前的石头就像一块变软了的黄油，亚瑟毫不费力地就把神剑拔出来，接着在凯伊跟前单膝跪下，此时大家正好赶了回来。

"他成功了，凯伊爵士是英格兰真正的国王！"亚瑟喊道。

所有人都拜倒在米格尔跟前，连梅林也不例外。

"等等。"

但没有人听见他的话。

人们齐声喊道："凯伊王万岁！"

---

treachery *n.* 背叛

One Man's Glory

Miguel looked out into the crowd. He could not deny that this respect felt great. But Merlin's eyes pierced into him, and his thoughts of glory *fizzled* like bubbles disappearing down a *drain*.

"Wait!" he cried. "I am not king!" He glanced around the crowd, but Arthur was nowhere to be found. "Where is my brother?"

"Arthur has begun the journey home to *notify* the kingdom," Sir Ector said.

"NO!" Miguel ran toward the royal procession. A long line of horses flowed along a dusty road, and the *rightful* king rode a white horse to lead the way.

"Arthur!" Miguel screamed, but he was too far away.

孤独的荣耀

米格尔看着人群，不可否认被人尊崇的感觉是如此神奇。但梅林炽烈的目光似乎带刺，使他觉得一切荣耀都像泡沫一样被一一刺破，顿时消失不见了。

"等等！"他大喊，"我不是国王！"他在人群中搜寻，却没有看到亚瑟，"我弟弟呢？"

"亚瑟去布告全国了，"埃克特爵士回答。

"不要！"米格尔冲出皇家队列，看到长长的马队行走在泥泞的路上，而未来的国王却骑着白马走在队伍的最前面。

"亚瑟！"米格尔高声喊道，但亚瑟已经走得很远了。

---

fizzle *v.* 失败　　　　　　　　　　　　drain *n.* 排水管
notify *v.* 告知　　　　　　　　　　　　rightful *adj.* 合法的

Miguel hopped into the driver's seat of a *carriage*, grabbed the *reins*, and rode hard. Soon Miguel approached Arthur. "Wait, please," he cried. "You are the rightful king!"

"I have no desire for that *title*," he said.

"You will become the mightiest king in all of England," Miguel said.

The white horse slowed.

"You will rule in a powerful kingdom called Camelot."

Arthur stopped.

"You will be most respected by all your knights." Miguel stopped too.

"Have you seen the future, Brother?"

米格尔跳上马车，拉起缰绳，拼命追赶。很快，米格尔便赶上亚瑟，"等等，你才是真正的国王！"他大喊。

"我不在乎当什么国王，"亚瑟回答。

"你会是英格兰最伟大的国王，"米格尔说。

白马放慢了步伐。

"你将会统治最强大的王国——卡米洛特王国。"

亚瑟停了下来。

"你将会得到所有骑士的拥戴。"米格尔也停了下来。

"哥哥，你能预测未来吗？"

---

carriage *n.* 四轮马车

title *n.* 头衔

rein *n.* 缰绳

Miguel smiled. "Sort of."

"But you are my brother, not the son of Merlin," Arthur said. "You do not know my future, for as only one man, I would never desire the responsibility of governing an entire kingdom. Now go become king; it's what you seem to desire most."

"I am not the true king!" Miguel shouted to the wind as Arthur rode off.

"I know, I took young Arthur from King Uther himself. It is his *destiny*." Merlin was suddenly sitting next to Miguel.

"Then why am I here?"

"可以这么说吧。"米格尔笑着说。

"但你是我的兄长，又不是梅林的儿子，"亚瑟说道，"你是不会预知我的未来的。仅仅凭一己之力，我无法承担起一国之君的重任。你回去做你的国王好了，你那么想登上王位。"

亚瑟骑着马从米格尔身边飞驰而过，米格尔在他身后高喊道："我不是真正的国王！"

梅林不知什么时候突然坐在米格尔旁边。他说："我知道，是我把亚瑟从尤瑟国王的皇宫抱走的，这是他的命运。"

"那我为什么会出现在这里？"

---

destiny *n.* 命运

"Only you can answer that," Merlin said, and with that *cryptic* statement the *wizard* vanished, leaving Miguel alone to his own destiny.

Share the Wealth

The center of Sir Ector's castle garden held a *labyrinth*, and all around flowers and vines grew into *swirling*, curving structures. Leaves rustled ahead of him, leading Miguel into the maze.

"Arthur?" he called out.

Dark clouds rushed in overhead. The air chilled. Excalibur sizzled next to him.

"只有你自己才知道答案。"梅林留下一句令人费解的话便神秘地消失了，只留下米格尔一个人思考怎样面对此时的命运。

共享荣华

在埃克特爵士城堡的花园中心有一个迷宫，鲜花和弯曲的树藤环绕其中，花草被修剪成一个个奇特的造型。米格尔随着树叶沙沙的响声，走进了这个迷宫。

"亚瑟？"他喊道。

突然，天上乌云密布，空气一下子变得凉飕飕的。米格尔身上的神剑竟然动了起来，咝咝作响。

---

cryptic *adj.* 隐秘的　　　　　　　　　　　wizard *n.* 男巫
labyrinth *n.* 迷宫　　　　　　　　　　　swirl *v.* 旋涡

He traveled deeper into the maze, following voices that seemed to come from its center. The day grew darker and *spookier*.

Miguel wanted to turn back, but he knew this story would never end unless he moved forward. The time had come to end this game. Now or never.

"Arthur, you must become king," he said. "It is the only way."

"And face men like you, who will always chase glory and steal and lie to achieve their ends?"

"I was wrong. I let the power of Excalibur *eclipse* my judgment. You are the true king." Miguel said. "It is your special gift of leadership that this country deserves."

他跟着迷宫里传来的声音，往更深处走去。迷宫里面越来越暗，非常恐怖。

米格尔很想回头，但他知道若不继续往前走，故事是不会结束的。是时候结束这个游戏了，这是唯一的机会。

"亚瑟，你一定要做国王，这是命中注定的。"他说。

"你自己就是个很好的例子，有谁能一辈子追求荣耀，或者通过窃取和说谎来达到目的呢？"

"我错了。神剑令我失去了判断力。你才是真正的国王。"米格尔说，"你极富领导天赋，这个国家应当由你来统治。"

---

spooky *adj.* 怪异的　　　　　　　　　　　　　　　eclipse *v.* 遮蔽

"I will not govern alone," Arthur stated. "I need men around me who are willing to be patient, tell me when I am being unfair, and forgive me when I choose the easy path over the *righteous* one."

Arthur placed his hand on Miguel's shoulder, as Miguel kneeled before him, placing Excalibur in his hands.

"All hail King Arthur!"

Merlin stood behind them. "To King Arthur!" He raised his *staff*. One glance in the wizard's eyes, and suddenly Miguel was back at the loft. He *scrambled* down the *ladder* and grabbed his favorite bat out of his bag.

　　"我不想独自统治这个国家，"亚瑟说，"我需要身旁有人耐心倾听，当我处事不公时能够提醒我，在我投机取巧时能够宽恕我。"

　　亚瑟把手放在米格尔肩上，米格尔则跪在他面前，把亚瑟神剑交到他手上。

　　"亚瑟王万岁！"

　　梅林站着他们后面，"亚瑟王万岁！"他一边高喊着，一边举起了他的魔棒。米格尔看了一眼巫师的眼睛，便突然回到了阁楼里，他走下楼梯，拿起包里最爱的球棒。

---

righteous *adj.* 正义的
scramble *v.* 爬行

staff *n.* 权杖
ladder *n.* 梯子

At the batting cages, Trevon stood tall with a wide *stance*. His fan club was nowhere in sight.

Miguel watched and waited.

Trevon swung at his last pitch, missed, and then turned and saw Miguel.

"I'm sorry," said Miguel.

"What for?" asked Trevon, kicking the end of his bat with the toe of his shoe. "I was the *jerk*. And I needed to be told I was being a jerk."

"I'm sorry I let my jealousy keep me from being happy about what a great *hitter* you are."

棒球场上，特雷文站稳正准备击球，他的球迷们正在注视着他。

米格尔也耐心地等待着他的表现。

特雷文挥出最后一棒，却没打到球。他转过身，看到米格尔就站在身后。

"对不起，"米格尔说。

"为什么这么说？"特雷文边问边用鞋尖踢了踢球棒。"我是个混蛋，应该有人告诉我，我就是个混蛋。"

"我很抱歉，我因为嫉妒你，才没有为你在场上的出色表现感到高兴。"

---

stance *n.* 准备击球姿势   jerk *n.* 混蛋

hitter *n.* 击球手

"I'm sorry too," Trevon said.

"Apology accepted," said Miguel.

"Yeah," said Trevon. "You want to take some practice *swings*? I'll give you a few *pointers*."

Miguel smiled, and retrieved his helmet.

"C'mon, let's bat."

"我也很抱歉。"特雷文说。

"接受道歉。"米格尔说。

"太好了，"特雷文喊，"你还想练习怎样挥棒吗？我可以给你一些建议。"

米格尔笑了笑，拿起了头盔。

"走吧，我们打球去。"

---

swing *n.* 挥杆动作   pointer *n.* 指示